YES,
but is it
good
for the
Jews?

YES,
but is it
good
for the
Jews?

A BEGINNER'S GUIDE, VOLUME 1

Jonny Geller

BLOOMSBURY

Published by Bloomsbury USA, New York
Distributed to the trade by Holtzbrinck Publishers

All papers used by Bloomsbury USA are natural, recyclable products made from wood grown in well-managed forests. The manufacturing processes conform to the environmental regulations of the country of origin.

Page 146 Illustration of the "Jewish Nose" reprinted by kind permission of Russ Woodrow of the University of Newcastle. Taken from George Jabet's *Notes on Noses* (published 1852, London).

Page 202 Lyrics reprinted by kind permisission of Tim Rice 1968 (*Joseph and the Amazing Technicolor Dreamcoat*).

Library of Congress Cataloging-in-Publication Data
Geller, Jonny.
Yes, but is it good for the Jews? : a beginner's guide /
by Jonny Geller. — 1st U.S. ed.
p. cm.
ISBN-13: 978-1-59691-205-2 (hardcover)
ISBN-10: 1-59691-205-7 (hardcover)
1. Jews — Humor. I. Title.
PN6231.J5G44 2006
828'.9203 — dc22
2006002765

First U.S. Edition 2006

1 3 5 7 9 10 8 6 4 2

Typeset by Attic

Printed in the United States of America by Quebecor World Fairfield

Anyone meshugge enough to call himself a Jew,
is a Jew.

—DAVID BEN-GURION,
first prime minister of Israel

For

Karen, Ben, and Joe

—good for this Jew

Introduction

ow often have you asked—but dared not utter out loud for fear of ridicule—whether something or other was Good for the Jews? The PATRIOT Act? Israel's withdrawal from Gaza? Celine Dion? How often, at the end of a long argument on Friedman economic theory or the real implications of the U.S. government's reluctance to join the Kyoto treaty on climate change, have you spoken, breathlessly, the words you knew were on everyone else's lips around that Shabbos dinner table: Yes, but is it Good for the Jews?

The wait is over. *Yes, But Is It Good for the Jews?* will help you through the quagmire of indecision. No longer will you need to think twice about which product to boycott, which film to avoid, or which celebrity to disparage. The results of a proven scientific theorem based on thousands of years of Jewish Learning (see author's note) will be laid bare to you in the forthcoming pages. Judology, the mathematical formula that definitively evaluates whether someone or something is Good for the Jews, is the tool by which Jewish enlightenment is reached. In Judology, we do not use the word *Bad*, merely *Not Good*—after all, we've had 5,000 years of bad things happening to us. Why not be a little more positive?

This first book of a fourteen-volume cycle of works will outline the basic principals of Judology using selected examples in alphabetical order to guide the novice in the practicalities of this science. To aid the serious student of Judology on his or her path (yes, women are allowed to delve into the secrets of this reclusive sect) to Perfect Understanding, the author has provided maps, graphs, lists, and discussion topics. As with all Jewish academic endeavor, we at the Judological Institute of Spiritual Mathematics, or JISM, welcome your input and refer you to our Web site, www.isitgoodforthejews.com, where discussion forums encourage debate on issues covered in the book.

Who is a Jew? The editor defines this as one who has at least one Jewish parent and/or grandparent. In fact, just use the Nuremberg Laws of 1935 as a reliable guide—if it was good enough for Hitler, it's good enough for us.

One final note: please do not borrow this book from a friend or a library, as borrowing is Not Good for the Jews. Buying is.

Author's Note

> As long as there have been Jews, there has been Judology.
>
> —Rabbi Chelm of Bratislaw,
> *Judaica Numerolis,* 1648

Judology is undeniably one of Western civilization's oldest branches of the sciences. This short book cannot hope to do justice to the libraries of scholarship on the subject. The author merely wishes to bring the principles and some applications to the forefront of interested, curious minds.

Judology, like all mystical philosophies, has had its critics. Described as "arcane, diffuse, and frustrating" by its bête noire, Professor Amos Avla (*Judology Is Fake*, Manischewitz Press, 1928), the science was driven underground for more than eighty years until the latter part of the twentieth century.

What is Judology? In brief, it is a cousin of mathematics, a sister to the Talmudic art of Gematriya—

apportioning numerical value to individual letters in the Torah and thereby giving them mystical significance—a third cousin of Kabbalah. It is at heart a spiritual guide to the complexities of Jewish Identity. Happily, this study, which was previously restricted to male Jews over the age of forty-seven who had undergone circumcision twice, is now open to you, the hungry reader.

The Judological Institute of Spiritual Mathematics (JISM) is, for the first time, prepared to share its mathematical formula with the outside world. This is a highly controversial move and a rift occurred during the Annual Conference of Judology in the fall of 2005, when Solomon Pinkas, the dean of the Solomon Pinkas Academy of Spiritual Mathematics (SPASM), expelled members who voted in favor of sharing our findings with the world. A schism in SPASM led to the formation of JISM in 2006. We at the Institute believe there is too much secrecy in this world and it is time for Jew and non-Jew to work together and join forces in the process of determining whether something is Good or Not Good for the Jews. Less *Opus Dei*, more *Och 'n' Vey*.

In his informative 1927 book, Professor Ivor Broygus, MBris, Yd, defines Judology as "the numerical attribution or evaluation of whether something, animate or inanimate, is Good for the Jews" (*Tzoyrus* by Broygus, Paranoid Press, 1927). The author owes a supreme debt of gratitude to this monumental work, now sadly out of print, and wishes to refer any complaint, charges of libel, upset, or accusations of defamation to be directed to the offices of Professor Broygus's publishers, Paranoid Press, 23 Gramercy Park, New York, NY 10002.

> —JG, March 2006 at his home
> in a secret location

How Jew Are You?

Before embarking on our journey, perhaps take a moment to answer the following questions to determine if you are GOOD FOR THE JEWS.

1. Your only daughter brings home her new boyfriend, and they declare their intention to wed in the traditions of her new man's family—those of the Native American tribe of the Cherokee. His name is Adahy, which means "lives in the woods." Do you:
   A. welcome them into your home, prepare a lovely meal, and quietly retire to the bathroom, where you slit your throat?
   B. announce you are changing your name too—to Sitting Shiva?
   C. accept the style of the wedding as long as you can choose the caterer?

2. It is Christmas time, and little Mendle, your five-year-old, asks you why Jews don't have Santa Claus. Do you:

  A. tell him in a kind, gentle voice that Santa Claus is in fact based on Baron Herman von Claus, a famous Bavarian anti-Semite who poisoned Jewish children?

  B. tell him: Santa Claus is a lie, but don't mention it to Justin at school or he will beat you to a pulp?

  C. tell him that you put a sign on the roof saying "Keep Out! Jews Live Here"?

3. You are invited to your boss's house for dinner. He is serving the hors d'oeuvres—melon and ham. Do you:

  A. discreetly slip the ham under the tablecloth when nobody is looking?

  B. convince yourself it must be kosher meat that just looks like ham and tastes like wurst?

  C. say loudly that you are Jewish and you have always suspected your white boss of being a racist, particularly since his rendition of Public Enemy's "Fight the Power" at last year's Xmas party?

4. Your favorite team is playing on Yom Kippur. Do you:

   A. ask yourself: what is Yom Kippur?

   B. pretend you have a headache and leave shul to watch it in the quiet and privacy of your own home?

   C. TiVo the game and watch it after the breaking of the Fast?

5. The Six-Day War is:

   A. the third Arab-Israeli conflict, conducted over six days in 1967.

   B. a normal working week.

   C. the usual timeline it takes to get over a fight with your spouse.

6. You are choosing a vacation. Do you:

   A. think about it, skim the brochures, and then book the Keys like every year?

   B. check out whether the country voted for or against the creation of Israel in 1948?

   C. not bother—the food is always awful, and they speak in such funny accents?

7. You have been invited to the bar mitzvah of the son of a relative you haven't spoken to for many years due to a family broygus, the cause of which you can't remember. Do you:

   A. attend the simcha and lavish generous gifts on the unsuspecting bar mitzvah boy?

   B. attend the function, eat and drink as much as you can, stuff your pockets full of leftovers and free cigars, and leave, giving him a crisp five-dollar bill?

   C. fall out with every family member over whether you should attend, induce an ulcer and insomnia, go and have a miserable time?

8. Hasidism is:

   A. a bunch of meshugganehs who screw through a sheet?

   B. a revolutionary movement founded in the eighteenth-century Pale of Settlement that introduced Joy to devotion in religious Judaism?

   C. I loved *Yentl*.

9. You are invited to join the local reading group, where you will be the only Jew in the club. Do you:

   A. say how much you loved *The Great Gatsby*, so everyone knows you are not too Jewish?

    B. say no to every suggestion until somebody eventually suggests either Primo Levi or Philip Roth?

    C. the price of books these days, I'd rather wait for the movie.

10. Circumcision is:

    A. a ritual that orginates with Abraham's covenant to God and a symbol of Jewish comittment to a spiritual life?

    B. a snip off the old block?

    C. very common these days. Which porn star can you name that hasn't been circumcised?

A = 3 points   *B = 5 points*   *C = 7 points*

If you scored between 30 and 40 points, you are NOT GOOD FOR THE JEWS. Do you mix enough with Jews? Why not join your local bridge club as a start?

If you scored 41 to 55 points, you are clearly a Jew with self-hating issues. You are NOT GOOD FOR THE JEWS. No advice available.

If you scored 56 to 70 points, you are a balanced, integrated Jew who is ready to enter the first stage of Judology. No advice needed.

The Mathematical Formula

Here, for the first time, the secret formula to determine whether something is Good or Not Good for the Jews will be revealed. It must be noted that if an entry is defined as Not Good, it does not necessarily mean that, as such, it is Bad for the Jews. It is merely not a positive force for Jews. In certain cases, it can simply be Jew-neutral and therefore simply Not Good and Not Bad.

Important Note

Each category is marked out of 7, the most important number for Jews. According to the Laws of Judology, the determination of how this mark out of 7 is reached can only be disclosed to someone who knows all six orders of Hillel's Mishnah—backward and in French. The number 7 is important in many religions, none more so than in Judaism. For example:

7 days in the week

7 planetary spheres

7 wonders of the world

7 fat cows eat *7* thin cows in Pharoah's dream

Moses wore size *7* sandals

7 deadly sins

7 graces

7-year itch

*7*th month in the Jewish calendar marks the start
of the New Year

7 seas

7 dwarfs

7 courses served in an average Jewish
Friday-night dinner

Formula

Anti-Semitic Potential (otherwise known as Backlash)#
+ Impact on the World ♨ x The J-Factor* = Tzurus°

Tzurus ÷ *7* (the mystical Kabbalistic number)[7] =

0–7 = Not Good for the Jews

7.1–7.99 = Borderline, so therefore probably Not Good
for the Jews

8–14 = Good for the Jews

So, for Example, Easter

7 (Anti-Semitic Backlash Potential) + 6.8 (Impact on the World) x 3.35 (The J-Factor) = 46.23 (Tzurus) ÷ 7 (Mystical Kabbalistic Number) = 6.6 (Good or Not Good for the Jews)

Therefore Easter is NOT GOOD FOR THE JEWS

Clearly there is anti-Semitic potential in everything, so this category is hard to evaluate. We have restricted this to mean an open and obvious threat to the Jews. So violence resulting from subject will score 7; a slight fear of anti-Semitic backlash will score 1. This will be known as "Backlash."

ש Lasting impact defined as being ten years or more if subject has spawned imitators/imitations or movements outside the orginal intended impact. Effect will be judged on impact outside the United States. This will be known as "Impact."

* Defined as having any link whatsoever to Jewish heritage, culture, or matrilineal descent or whether the subject is open about his or her Jewishness or if subject is known as being particularly "Jewish." The higher the grade, the more overt the Jewish identity. We have refused to look back further than seven generations. This will be known as "The J-Factor."

^o *Tzurus* is Yiddish for "troubles," the default position of world Jewry. Tzurus is the effect of backlash potential spread across the world having increased by Jewish origin.

[7]The mystical Kabbalistic number 7 will be known as "Kabbalah."

Alcohol According to Fogwell's *Guides*, alcoholic liquor is one of the basic constituents of wine. Alcohol is a tasteless and colorless chemical that occurs naturally during fermentation when sugars from grape juice are processed by yeast. The alcohol content of wine ranges from about 8 percent to 14 percent by volume.

Wine and religion have a long history together. Many medieval monks throughout Europe had a major sideline as vintners. Jews are commanded to have at least four full cups on Passover (some argue that it is the only way to get through the interminable Seder service), and on Purim (the festival to commemorate the survival of Jews from genocide)

Jews are ordered to get as drunk as skunks. The commandment on Purim is quite specific: no beer or spirits, just wine, and only at the daytime Purim meal. One custom even decrees that a Jew should drink "until he does not know" the difference between Mordechai (the loyal leader) and Haman (the evil tyrant). If every time Jews commemorated escape from near-extinction by getting drunk, there would be a lot of pissed Jews on the subway.

A story: Rabbi Samuelson crashes into the car of Father Mulranney. Miraculously, neither cleric sustains any injury. In fact, not a scratch is to be found on either of them. Both cars are wrecks. "Surely, a sign from Hashem," Rabbi Samuelson declares. "To be true—the hand of God," agrees Father Mulranney. "Even more miraculous," says the rabbi, "is this unbroken bottle of kosher wine in my boot." He opens the wine and passes it to the priest, who takes a few swigs. The rabbi then throws the bottle away. "You're not having any?" the priest asks. "Nah, I'll wait until the police come," the rabbi answers.

Aside from the Purim clause, the Bible takes a rather unsympathetic view of alcohol. Drunkenness was punishable by death (Deuteronomy 21:20–21); Lot was seduced by his own daughters when they'd had a few too many Tia Marias (Genesis 19:33–36); King Solomon the Wise was convinced his wisdom came from a bottle, so he was shicker a lot, poor fellow; Noah got so drunk that when he was discovered naked by his son Ham, the unlucky boy was cursed; Aaron's two sons were killed for officiating as priests while drunk; and so on.

For non-Jews it is different. Jesus turns water into wine at Cana (John 2), and thus begins two millennia of alcoholism among priests. Traditionally, Jewish member-only golf clubs demand higher fees to compensate for the lack of income they would normally get from non-Jews at the bar. If you read the Bible, wouldn't you be terrified of drinking?

One true story: a Hasidic rabbi invites a new member to his home for Shabbos dinner after the service. The rabbi is widely known for his piety and his absolute belief that every commandment in the Torah must be practiced. The rabbi offers the new congregant a whiskey before the meal; the member declines politely, saying: "Sorry, Rabbi, I'm driving." Sometimes, a Jew should shut up and drink.

backlash	impact	j-factor	tzurus	kabbalah	good/not good
3.1 +	7 x	4.5	= 45.45 ÷	7 =	6.49

Alcohol is NOT GOOD FOR THE JEWS

....

Amish, the A Christian sect of about 145,000 people who live in settlements across the United States and in Ontario, Canada, but are found mostly in Pennsylvania, Ohio, and Indiana. They are the descendents of Swiss Anabaptists (later known as Mennonites) who broke from the church to follow Jacob Ammam in the 1600s. They moved to America in the eighteenth and nineteenth centuries to escape hard times and persecution in Europe. They will not embrace modernity. They speak a dialect of German called Pennsylvania Dutch. (source: padutch.com)

The Amish and the Hasidim have much in common. Both share a penchant for the ancient art of facial hair sculpting and both have been depicted in mainstream cinema. The Amish were portrayed sympathetically in *Witness* (1985), featuring the sumptuous Kelly McGillis. The Hasidim were depicted shamefully in that dreck movie *A Stranger Among Us* (1992), with the pneumatic Melanie Griffith. Hardly a fair fight.

The similarity in looks between the Lubavitchers and the Amish can be of use if you happen to be a Hasid being chased down a Pennsylvanian street by a horde of Jew-haters. Shout a few choice phrases in Pennsylvania Dutch to distract your pursuers, and they will stop in their tracks and offer to help you onto the back of your horse and cart.

Consider this famous story: a woman on a bus in the Midwest was overheard abusing a young man, dressed in black hat, black coat, and long, dark beard, who happened to sit next to her. "Tut-tut. Jews like you," she spat. "I'm sorry, madam?" he said. "Look at you—with your thick, black coat in the height of summer and your ridiculous hat! It's Jews like you that give the rest of us a bad name." He replied modestly, "I beg your pardon, madam, but I am not Jewish. I'm Amish." The woman looked back and smiled, "How nice. You've kept your customs."

backlash		impact		j-factor		tzurus		kabbalah		good/not good
3.7	+	2.2	x	2	=	11.8	÷	7	=	1.7

The Amish are NOT GOOD FOR THE JEWS

Ashamed of Your Name?
Jews Who Switched

Cardinal Jean-Marie Lustiger changed his name from **Aaron Lustiger**. Yes, the former Archbishop of Paris is in fact a Jew. For a moment, the World's First Bona Fide Jewish Pope was a possibility. Sadly, the non-Jewish German Joseph Ratzinger beat him to the post after Cardinal Lustiger's mentor, John Paul II, died in 2005.

Robert Zimmerman changed his name to **Bob Dylan** when he realized the closest thing to Jewish folk music was klezmer, and there ain't no money in klezmer. He also changed religions for a brief spell when he became a born-again Christian in 1979. This proved a bad career move, as his two "Christian albums," *Slow Train Coming* and *Saved*, were, well, shit. Religiously he redeemed himself with his pro-Israel song "Neighborhood Bully" on the 1983 album *Infidels*. He was later photographed at the Western Wall in Jerusalem wearing a skullcap.

Albert Einstein changed his name to **Albert Brooks**. No, not that Albert Einstein. What kind of parent does this to a son? Nobody can blame Albert Brooks, the actor, writer, and director (*Broadcast News*, *The Muse*) for changing his surname. It is doubtful that this was motivated by shame of being Jewish—more likely by fear of daily humiliation on the playground.

Melvin Kaminsky changed his name to **Mel Brooks**. **Allen Stewart Königsberg** changed his name to **Woody Allen**. Makes sense—after all, the last thing these young comedians needed was people thinking they were Jewish. No future in that.

Ralphie Lifshitz changed his name to **Ralph Lauren**. The son of a house painter, young Ralphie realized early on that there was no future in fashion with a dentist's name. Imagine people buying Dolce and Gabinski or Georgio Armanilovitch. Doesn't work.

Jonathan Stuart Leibowitz clearly felt it paid to sound Scottish rather than Jewish; he discreetly removed the conspicuous surname to become **Jon Stewart** and found fame on *The Daily Show* as a result.

Leonard Alfred Schneider changed his name to **Lenny Bruce** because he thought Schneider was "too Hollywood."

Issur Danielovich Demsky changed his name to **Kirk Douglas,** which is probably the most dramatic name switch in history, as "Kirk" means "Church."

Paul Simon and **Art Garfunkel** did not change their names! Perhaps they thought referring to Jesus in their hit song "Mrs. Robinson" might get them off the hook? Their first hit was, however, under the pseudonym of Tom and Jerry, but their Columbia Records producer Tom Wilson was furious when they suggested that their names were too Jewish. He insisted they couldn't sing about racial injustice and not appear "too Jewish."

Bagel, the A bread product made from yeasted wheat dough shaped as a ring that is boiled and then baked. The bagel is said to have originated in 1683, when a Jewish baker from Vienna created it as a gift to King Jan Sobieski of Poland to commemorate the king's victory over the Turks in that year. Immigrants in the 1880s brought the bagel to New York City, where it continues to be very popular, as it does nationwide.

The bagel is clearly the greatest export for the Jews since the Old Testament. In Russia, the *bublik* has become so mainstream that most Russians aren't aware that it was originally a Jewish bread. The fact that people in many countries that are steeped in anti-

Semitism enjoy the bagel and do not know it was created, developed, and distributed by Jews makes this category all the sweeter.

The bagel has also been a symbol of philosophical difference. Rabbi Plotz of Pinsk, the famous biblical commentator, said, "The non-Jew sees the bagel, the Jew sees the hole." However, it has been pointed out that the baker charges for the bagel, hole or no hole.

backlash	impact	j-factor	tzurus	kabbalah		good/not good
3.05	+ 5.45	x 6.9	= 58.65 +	7	=	8.38

The bagel is GOOD FOR THE JEWS

Bee, the National Spelling Administered by E. W. Scripps, the National Spelling Bee is in its seventy-ninth year. A national institution, this annual event was first introduced in 1925 and is now so popular that it is televized and attracts a huge audience. Contestants must be fourteen or younger and must first win their state championships before they can go on to represent their state at the national competition. The 1999 Bee was covered in the Oscar-nominated documentary *Spellbound*, directed by Jeff Blitz.

The National Spelling Bee is screened on ESPN, so it must be a sport—and a sport Jews can actually win! All it needs is the magic Jewish combination of a nerdy, bookish prepubescent and a very pushy parent. Slam dunk, if you ask me. For the spectator, there is also the added joy in seeing a Gentile from Iowa really, really trying to spell the word "Lubavitcher." Judologists take the Spelling Bee extremely seriously as a recruiting ground for potential candidates for the Judological Institute of Spiritual Mathematics (JISM), as we are always on the hunt for students of the Word. If every letter in the Torah has numerical significance and every word several meanings, then spelling is pretty important to the Jews.

It is not all one way, and Jews' knowledge of their host nation and culture is also tested. In some ways, the Spelling Bee can be seen as a subtle, coded, discreet way of testing citizenship. For example, was there an anti-Semitic agenda when Harry, a Jewish kid from New Jersey, was eliminated from the competition after he failed to spell the word "banns" correctly in the documentary *Spellbound*? How was he to know this word for the religious announcement of a marriage—a word that orginated in the Catholic Church?

For those worried about an Aryan slant to the questions, recall that the 1983 final word was "Purim" (somethingjew ish.co.uk). But anyone who cannot spell this word, denoting the time when Jews were threatened with annihilation, might well be an anti-Semite. Sensitivities reached fever pitch when the *San Francisco Chronicle* got into trouble after publishing a test poster for the Bee. In test example number 10, the word "disproportionate" was used in the following context: "Israel came under heavy international criticism for the Gaza offensive. UN Secretary-General Kofi Annan and others questioned whether it had been a disproportionate response to the use of crude Qassam rockets by Palestinian militants." Jewish groups clearly saw this as a coded calling card for Hamas. The paper later apologized.

backlash	impact	j-factor	tzurus	kabbalah	good/not good
5.04 +	5.4 x	6.2 =	64.7 ÷	7 =	9.25

The National Spelling Bee is GOOD FOR THE JEWS

Bewitched Over 250 episodes of this sitcom ran from 1964 to 1972. Samantha (Elizabeth Montgomery) and Darrin (Dick York and Dick Sargent) are a nondescript couple living in a Connecticut suburb, she a housewife, he an advertising executive. Samantha is a witch, but she promises her husband that she will not use her magic at home and will be a good, normal wife. She proves unable to do this, as her numerous eccentric relatives pop in to cause chaos in every episode. In 2005 a movie version was released with Nicole Kidman as Samantha, Will Ferrell as Darrin, and Shirley MacLaine as Samantha's mother, Endora.

Exodus 22:18: "Thou shalt not suffer a witch to live."

Bewitched is the prototype of all American sitcoms. It also presents a fascinating dilemma for the Judologist. An assimilationist fantasy or a Jewish expression of identity? America was still reeling from the effects of McCarthyism when *Bewitched* began production, and Jewish writers had to be careful how they expressed their views, so it is worth examining the possible subtext or semiotics of this groundbreaking sitcom.

Assimilationist Fantasy

Although no Jewish actors appeared on-screen in the main roles, *Bewitched* was created by Sol Saks and directed by William Asher (other Jewish writers and directors on the show included Ron Friedman, Bernie Kahn, Milt Rosen, Jack Sher, Fred Freeman and Lawrence J. Cohen, Jerry Mayer and Paul L. Friedman, Sherman Marks, Alan Rafkin, and R. Robert Rosenbaum—even the recent movie was written, directed, and produced by Jews).

William Asher was married to Elizabeth Montgomery (Samantha), and the sight of the small, balding Jewish-boy-made-good together with the slender, WASPish, all-American blond, Ms. Montgomery, could be mistaken for a picture from the pages of *Der Stürmer*.

Marrying out has never looked so good.

In post-fifties America, the Great Jewish American

Dream was the picket fence, the job in advertising or insurance, and the shiksa wife waiting at home. There are even the slightly annoying next-door Jews, Gladys and Abner Kravitz, to make the picture perfect. Jews should be close but not too close. However, the hidden subtext is that the lovely blond at home is in fact a witch. Being accepted is hard. In the episode "The Battle of Burning Oak," the chairman of the exclusive Burning Oak country club proposes Darrin for membership, but Samantha's humble ancestry ruins their chances of breaking into this American purebred elite. A heartbreaking cri de coeur of the Jewish Experience?

Jewish Expression of Identity

On the other hand, perhaps Samantha is the Jew? From Darrin's point of view, he has an overbearing mother-in-law who is a big macher in the witches' community. She disapproves greatly of his marriage to her daughter, she hates seeing Samantha suppressing her witch identity to fit in with her mortal husband (read *goy*) and his mortal concerns (gaining membership at exclusive clubs). Samantha just wants to be like everyone around her and for people to accept her as one of them. Trouble is, her community, her family, her heritage, and her own innate witchness just keep surfacing. And when her children are born, there is no denying that they have inherited her powers—matrilineal descent.

Remember too that her power resides in her nose.

Bewitched also contains a misogynist subliminal message, namely, you keep your wife stuck in the kitchen for long enough, she turns into a witch—and worse, her mother.

backlash	impact	j-factor	tzurus	kabbalah	good/not good
4.68 +	3.4 x	5.7 =	46.1 ÷	7 =	6.6

Bewitched *is NOT GOOD FOR THE JEWS*

....

Bible, the: Old Testament Written between 1400 and 100 BC, the Old Testament (also called the Hebrew Bible or Tanakh) is a collection of five books of Moses, eight books of Prophets, and eleven books of writings. The Pentateuch, or Chumash, consists of the principal five books of Moses, which detail the story of the Hebrews as they left slavery and founded their own country in Israel, the land promised to them by God, according to the Torah. The Creation of the World is described in the first book, Genesis.

....

Without these books, there would be no Jews, so it is hard to argue that the five books of Moses are Bad for the Jews. The 613 commandments, however, are way too many rules—248 laws dictating what you should do, and 365 saying what you can't. No wonder Jews have been criticized for being bossy control freaks. With that much *nudjing*, who wouldn't be a bag of nerves?

Also, the laws on animal sacrifice are excessive in this day and age.

Terms like "Chosen People" do not help either.

backlash	*impact*	*j-factor*	*tzurus*	*kabbalah*	*good/not good*
7 +	7 x	7 =	98 ÷	7 =	14

The Old Testament is GOOD FOR THE JEWS

Bible, the: New Testament The New Testament, or Greek Scriptures, is a collection of twenty-seven books written after the life of Jesus Christ. The New Testament was written over a one hundred-year period between AD 50 and AD 150 and covers the life and teachings of the Son of God, according to the Christian Bible. There are many authors of these books, but the primary sources are the Gospels written by Matthew, Mark, Luke, and John.

Jesus was a Jew and was named the Jewish King even at his crucifixion, so there are strong arguments to defend the New Testament's place in the pro-Jew pantheon, but troublesome sections such as Matthew 27:25, which states, "Then answered all the people, and said, His blood be on us, and on our children," and John 19:6, 15, which shows the Jews shouting "crucify him," did not help the successful integration of the Jewish people into the Christian world.

However, the authors of the Gospels—with the possible exception of Luke—were all Jews, so unless they were the first self-haters in history, they could just have been complaining about the Jewish authorities rather than Jews as a whole. Many notable passages ascribe blame for Jesus's execution to the Jewish Sanhedrin, so maybe the fault does lie with the administration. Having said this, the Roman procurator Pontius Pilate is portrayed as a puppet of the unruly Jewish crowd and the powerful Jewish lobby who were bent on shaping policy to suit their own nefarious ends. Some things don't change.

Jews in the New Testament do not come out of it well unless they are converting to Christianity, otherwise it is said that "salvation is from the Jews" (John 4:22). Hard to argue that the Good News Bible is Great News for the Jews.

backlash   *impact*   *j-factor*   *tzurus*   *kabbalah*   *good/not good*

backlash		impact		j-factor		tzurus		kabbalah		good/not good
7	+	5	x	3.5	=	42	÷	7	=	6

The New Testament is NOT GOOD FOR THE JEWS

Cheesecake A dessert with a creamy cheese filling atop a crust of some sort. The typical cheesecake uses cream cheese and a graham cracker crust, but you can create many varieties by adding other ingredients such as nuts, chocolate, or fruit, using different types of cheese, using different types of base, or cooking for different lengths of time. Cheesecake was served to athletes during the first Olympic Games in 776 BC. The Romans then took cheesecake from Greece to Europe, and centuries later, European immigrants brought cheesecake to America.

Is there a spiritual quality to cheesecake? It is the dish of the Jewish festival Shavuot, when Jews commemorate the giving of the Ten Commandments to Moses and the Israelites. Why did the starving, overheated Jews want cheesecake, of all things, to celebrate this turning point in their history?

Cheese makes important appearances in the Bible. One of the many names for Mount Sinai in Hebrew is Bar Gavnunim (mountain of peaks), the same root as *gevinah*, the word for cheese. Some speculate that the Israelites had left camp for so long to listen to all the new rules that their milk turned sour and became cheese (source: *The Jewish Journal of Los Angeles*, 2002). Whatever the case, it would make more sense for us to eat cheese balls or cheese souffle rather than cheesecake, wouldn't it?

Cheese has also been key to fighting. Cheese is mentioned in the Bible (I Samuel 1:17–18) when a young shepherd boy brings some ten cheeses to the battlefield to feed the soldiers who were fighting the mighty Philistines. The young man bringing this important food? David, the slayer of the giant Goliath and Israel's second King.

The role of cheese in defeating Israel's enemies does not end there. Judith defeated Holofernes in the Book of Judith by feeding him salty cheese. The cunning vixen knew that his fromage-induced thirst would create a craving for wine (which she happened to have at the ready by the bedside), which made him sleepy, which allowed Judith to chop off his head and save the Jews from this homicidal general in Nebuchadnezzar's army. Cheese and wine parties will never be the same.

Indeed, the U.S. Army recognizes the strange hold cheese has over the Jews and, with the assistance of the Aleph Institute (Florida), issues to all observant Jewish servicemen overseas a portion of cheesecake. Before they invented the "shelf stable" product that does not need refrigeration, this practice might have led to disaster. Some have argued that the stink of the melted cheesecakes contributed to the defeat in Vietnam.

For the lactose-intolerant, and there are many in the Jewish community, cheesecake is torture and should be avoided. It is also so rich that it contributes to heart attacks.

backlash		impact		j-factor		tzurus		kabbalah		good/not good
1.45	+	3.5	x	6.15	= 30.44	÷	7		=	4.35

Cheesecake is NOT GOOD FOR THE JEWS

- -

Cholera Originated on the Indian subcontinent; the bacteriologist Robert Koch (1843–1910) identified the *Vitrio cholerae* bacterium that causes this infectious disease. Cholera is passed from human to human by drinking water or eating food contaminated with the bacterium. In an epidemic, the source of the contamination is usually the feces (stool) of an infected person. In the United States, cholera was prevalent in the 1800s but has been virtually eliminated by modern sewage and water treatment systems. Like most great pestilences, Jews have been blamed for bringing Cholera to the world. The great Hamburg epidemic of 1892 was blamed on Jews from the East (Ostjuden); in the same year, the Ostjuden were blamed for bringing cholera and typhus to New York, causing President Benjamin Harrison to halt immigration into the country. This closed the door to many Jews fleeing the pogroms in Russia.

Tell me, who is cholera good for exactly?

backlash		impact		j-factor		tzurus		kabbalah		good/not good
7	+	5	x	0	=	0	÷	7	=	0

Cholera is NOT GOOD FOR THE JEWS

Cholesterol According to the American Heart Association, cholesterol is a waxy substance found in the blood-stream and in the body's cells. It is healthy in small amounts. A high level of cholesterol in the blood is a major risk factor for coronary heart disease, which leads to heart attack. It's also a risk factor for stroke. Hypercholesterolemia is the term for high levels of blood cholesterol. Cholesterol is generated in the body and is found in foods such as fish, meat, eggs, cheese, butter, and milk. Food from plants—like fruits, vegetables, and cereals—doesn't contain cholesterol.

....

Cholesterol is not a great friend to the Jewish lover of food. Strudel, cholent, salt beef, cheesecake, chopped liver—mainstays of the Jewish home—all contain low-density lipoprotein (LDL) which clogs your arteries. "Feh!" you might say, if you are one of the many East European Ashkenazi Jewish centenarians brought up on a rich, cholesterol-high diet. Some recent studies have supported the heredity argument: a variant form has been found of a gene called CETP; this gene encodes the cholesteryl ester transfer protein (CETP), which helps form and move cholesterol particles around the body, and the variant may be linked to longevity. Even better news came when it was reported that some genetic variations benefit a Jewish population and might not occur in other ethnic groups (source: *Science News*, volume 164).

Does that mean Jews can gorge themselves on tzimmes and potato kugel while non-Jews have to become vegetarians? Could this finally be the reason why Jews are the Chosen People? Unlikely. Remember, Jews are commanded to "watch yourselves very carefully" (Deuteronomy 4:15), and with the mad cow disease and Asian bird flu scares, it might be time for Jews to give up their triple-decker deli sandwiches and get excited by parsnips and broccoli. Heart disease in particular kills 50 percent of Americans, and that includes Jewish Americans.

A Jewish breakthrough in the fight against cholesterol came by way of Dr. Shela Gorinstein, who helped develop the hybrid fruit called pomelit, which can significantly lower cholesterol levels. Two Jews won the Nobel Prize for their work on regulating cholesterol (Michael S. Brown and Joseph L. Goldstein, 1985). So Jews are Not Good for cholesterol.

backlash		impact		j-factor		tzurus		kabbalah		good/not good
1.5	+	6.4	x	4.8	=	37.9	÷	7	=	5.4

Cholesterol is NOT GOOD FOR THE JEWS

Colonic Irrigation (also called Colonics and Colon Hydrotherapy) A procedure where warm water is pumped into the intestinal tract through a rubber tube that is inserted twenty inches into the patient's backside. Sometimes the water is spiked with special herbs, or wheatgrass extract, or other substances to help the flow. Also known as "autointoxication" theory, the practice can be traced back to the ancient Egyptians and led to the popularity of colonic irrigation as a supposed cure. One of its major champions was John Harvey Kellogg, the health-food pioneer.

Marilyn Monroe once confided to her psychiatrist, Dr. Ralph Greenson, that Mae West was given an enema every day and said it kept her young. West also recommended one orgasm a day, but that doesn't fit into this entry, as it were.

What does colonic irrigation have to do with the Jews? According to the Bible (and Dr. Jerry Glenn Knox, author of *Love Thine Enemas and Heal Thyself*) the colon is the seat of the personality. It is said that constipated people are nervous, irritable, and hard to get along with. People with good bowel function tend to be congenial, relaxed, and more "at home with themselves." Clearly it would be a massive generalization to say Jews are uptight, irritable, and nervy, but there has been a sharp rise in colonic therapy within the Jewish community in recent years.

Scientists have argued that a large colon can be inherited and is common among some ethnic groups, such as Ashkenazi Jews. Dr. Knox relates the story of a patient who would "go up to eleven days between bowel movements . . . She had a massive colon. I believe this is the reason that many Ashkenazis have a syndrome in which they have idiopathic abdominal pain." In other words, Jews simply don't need to defecate as much as non-Jews, but they sure like to complain about it. Famously, Jack Osbourne, son of Sharon and Ozzy Osbourne, underwent a weeklong, twice-daily regime of colonic irrigation and lost ten pounds and weaned himself off booze and drugs—an appealing prospect for Jews who wish to let it all hang out and fight off the effects of too much lokshen pudding.

World Timeline
(Part I—from the Creation to Jesus)

World				
4.55 billion years BC	150,000 BC	50,000 BC	3760 BC	1875 BC–1445
Earth formed	First signs of *Homo sapiens* found	Man arrives in Europe	Jewish calendar begins	Egyptians ens Israelites

Jewish				
4.55 billion years BC	150,000 BC	50,000 BC	3760 BC	1875 BC–1445
No, the world was created 5,767 years ago	Nonsense, the world was created 5,767 years ago	Oy ya broch, THE WORLD WAS CREAT-ED 5,767 years ago	At last, someone believes me!	Bad job prospe for Jews

ere are two brief timelines running concurrently to aid Judologists who would like to refresh their memory of past events that were Good for the Jews and those we wish to forget. The author wants to make it clear that this is not definitive.

1444 BC–800 BC	776 BC	600 BC–500 BC	100 BC–AD 100
First code of laws	Olympic Games	Babylon destroys Temple (586)	Jesus born and died
Moses frees Jews			Romans destroy Temple (AD 70)
Solomon builds Temple in Jerusalem		Democracy develops in Athens	

1444 BC–800 BC	776 BC	600 BC–500 BC	100 BC–AD 100
First lawyer paid	No interest to Jews	Jerusalem house prices plummet	Our tzurus begins
Lots of Jews wandering			Tzurus increases
Jerusalem house prices shoot up		Jews have more opinions	

Vichy, in France, is famous for its mud baths and colonic treatments. However, improving the residents' bowel functions did not seem to relax the townspeople's attitude to Jews when they collaborated with Hitler in 1940.

backlash		impact		j-factor		tzurus		kabbalah		good/not good
3	+	3.3	x	1.5	= 9.45	÷	7		=	1.35

Colonic irrigation is NOT GOOD FOR THE JEWS

Complaining Webster's dictionary defines the verb *complain* as "to express grief, pain, or discontent or to make a formal accusation or charge." *Kvetch* is the Yiddish word for this term. Woody Allen defined kvetching with this joke: Two old yentas are sitting in a restaurant. "The food here is just awful." The other agrees, "Yes, and such small portions."

It is not just anti-Semites who have given the Jews cause to grumble. They manage quite well on their own. One could read the book of Exodus as one long gripe as the Jews escape slavery and wander through the desert to freedom—the food is no good (manna), nobody listens to us (golden calf), this long schlep and *fur wus*? In Egypt, they might have beaten us black and blue and raped our daughters, but at least the trains ran on time, et cetera. Mind you, forty years, by anyone's standards, is a long time to go property hunting, and their boss did go off for long periods with no word.

All cultures complain. Is campaigning for civil rights complaining? Is marching against the war in Iraq complaining? Is asking for a decent portion instead of this vershimmalte excuse for a brisket of lamb complaining? Is writing endless letters to the *New York Times* about its coverage of Israel complaining? As someone famously said, "To err is human, to complain divine." But there is something uniquely Jewish about complaining. For example, two famous stories to show the difference in ethnic complaining:

Grandma Esti is playing with her beloved grandson, Heskell, on the beach when a huge wave comes and snatches him out to sea. "*A klog iz mir!*" she screams. "*Got in himl*, save my little Heskell! I'll do anything—go to shul more, I'll even keep kosher! I beg of you, bring him back." Suddenly, the rage of the sea quiets and, as if by miracle, the little boy is delivered to her on the seashore. Grandma Esti looks up to the skies and says: "And the hat?"

A devout Christian joins a monastery, a new order where the vow of silence is broken only every seven years, when he will be allowed to say two words. After the first seven years, he is summoned to the abbott, Brother Augustus, and quietly says his two words. "Very drafty." Brother Augustus nods. Seven more years pass. The young man coughs and whispers his words, "Hard floor." Brother Augustus nods. Seven more years pass. "I quit," he says. Brother Augustus sighs and says, "Well, that's no surprise, you've done nothing but complain since the moment you got here."

Perhaps complaining is a survival instinct?

backlash		impact		j-factor		tzurus		kabbalah		good/not good
4.25	+	4.35	x	6.85	= 58.91	÷	7		=	8.41

Complaining is GOOD FOR THE JEWS

Deep Throat (the Man) William Mark Felt Sr. (born August 17, 1913) was second in command at the FBI during the Watergate investigations; he was also the main informant to the *Washington Post* of the link between the Watergate Hotel break-in and the White House. He was known to the newspaper as Deep Throat, so-called by reporter Bob Woodward to keep his identity secret. The information he supplied led to the resignation of President Richard M. Nixon in 1974. His identity was finally revealed in 2005 by his family in an article in *Vanity Fair* magazine.

W. Mark Felt is the man who brought down that Republican mamzer Nixon. The man surely must be Good for the Jews?

The fact that Nixon suspected he was Jewish adds a large dose of schadenfreude as well. According to the *Washington Post*, Nixon inquired as to Felt's religion and exclaimed: "[Expletive], [the bureau] put a Jew in there?" To which his chief of staff, Bob Haldeman, responded, "Well, that could explain it."

However, Mr. Felt is not Jewish but of Irish descent and claims no religious affiliation. People might *think* he is Jewish because of his Jewish-sounding name and might blame the Jews for meddling with the FBI and betraying the president. Added to this, Nixon was busy trying to help Israel during its toughest war, the Yom Kippur War in 1973, so one could argue that any distraction from this was Not Good for the Jews.

Traitor or hero?

Felt's name might sound Jewish, but does he look Jewish? The pictures taken outside his home on the day of the publication of the *Vanity Fair* article made him look more like one of those old Nazi war criminals one finds hanging out in Bolivia than the shammus at one's local shul.

backlash		*impact*		*j-factor*		*tzurus*		*kabbalah*		*good/not good*
6.24	+	4.17	x	2	= 20.82	÷	7	=		2.97

Deep Throat (the Man) is NOT GOOD FOR THE JEWS

***Deep Throat* (the Movie)** Released in the summer of 1972, written and directed by Gerard Damiano, and starring Linda Lovelace, *Deep Throat* was the first pornographic movie to be shown in many mainstream movie theaters.

Deep Throat is about a young woman (Linda Lovelace) who discovers that her clitoris is located in her throat; she can achieve orgasm only by "deep-throating" men, thereby achieving contact with her elusively placed genitalia.

Harry Reems "shot to fame" playing the doctor who helps his patient "come to her senses." He was the first Hebrew in history to be known for the size of his putz. The outrageous profit made on this skin flick (it cost $25,000 to make and grossed $600 million) was rumored to have been pocketed by Colombian mob lords, but there was very little involvement by Jews in the making of this movie. In the documentary on *Deep Throat* (*Inside Deep Throat*, February 2005), virtually all of the contributors are Jewish (Annie Sprinkle, Al Goldstein, Alan Dershowitz, Dr. Ruth Westheimer), which gives the impression that the movie was a Jewish event. This is patently untrue. After all, which Jewish movie would wax lyrical about an act unperformed in any Jewish household? On the other hand, as a wish-fulfillment fantasy, *Deep Throat* scores high for being Good for Jews.

However, one can see the movie as a treatise on disability—for what else is a clitoris in your throat other than a physical impairment?—and as such it is neither Good nor Bad for the Jews.

In 2005, a Swedish study by Kerstin Rosenquist at Malmö University found a link between oral sex and mouth cancer. Proof, finally, that Mother knows best.

backlash		impact		j-factor		tzurus		kabbalah		good/not good
4.5	+	4.25	x	5.75	= 50.31	÷	7	=		7.18

Deep Throat *(the Movie), is borderline and therefore NOT GOOD FOR THE JEWS*

Desperate Housewives ABC's hit show *Desperate Housewives* is described on its Web site as "a primetime soap with a truly contemporary take on 'happily every after,'" which takes a "darkly comedic look at suburbia, where the secret lives of housewives aren't always what they seem." It is narrated from the grave by Mary Alice, who committed suicide at the start of the first season, which aired in October 2004. She tells the stories of the friends and family she left behind on Wisteria Lane and the very dark undercurrent that runs beneath the surface of picture-perfect suburban life.

Desperate Housewives stars Teri Hatcher, Felicity

Huffman, Marcia Cross, Eva Longoria, and Nicollette Sheridan, and was created by Marc Cherry.

....

Without a single Jewish character or plotline, *Desperate Housewives* must be seen as a minimal threat to the Jews. However, most of the production team and writers are Jewish, and the concept of a "desperate housewife" was identified by a Jewish feminist, Betty Friedan, in her classic book, *The Feminine Mystique*. Also, Eva Longoria (Gabrielle Solis) did make her theatrical debut in *What the Rabbi Saw*.

Some have been angered by the show's moral ambiguity. A furor was kicked up when ABC ended its Easter Sunday tradition of airing the classic 1956 film *The Ten Commandments* in 2005 so *Desperate Housewives* could run in prime time. Scrapping the great biblical epic which shows the Jews defeating the Egyptians was undoubtedly a highly controversial act of aggression. The Easter 2005 episode was the most watched program in the United States—with more than 24 million viewers tuning in. Perhaps to this MTV generation, the sight of Moses smashing the tablets while the Israelites worship the golden calf cannot compete with the sight of Lynette swallowing pills while Gabrielle humps the gardener? Tough, but sometimes religion has to take a back seat.

Plans were announced in September 2005 to dub the series in Spanish for the potential 11 million Hispanic viewers in the United States. The Yiddish version is still under discussion, with ABC executives favoring the title "*Shtupping Shiksas.*"

backlash	impact	j-factor	tzurus	kabbalah		good/not good
3.45	+ 5.05	x 3.24	= 27.54	÷	7 =	3.93

Desperate Housewives *is NOT GOOD FOR THE JEWS*

Disney, Walt (born December 5, 1901, in Chicago, Illinois) A cartoonist who won fame and fortune in the entertainment industry through his films, television series, and theme parks. Disney became interested in drawing at a young age and went to Hollywood in 1923. With his brother Roy as business manager, he opened a studio and they produced a series of cartoons featuring a character called Oswald the Rabbit. When sound was introduced to film in 1927, Walt invented Mickey Mouse and provided the character's voice himself. By 1966, the year of his death, he had made some of the most successful children's movies of all time—*Bambi*, *Mary Poppins*, *Snow White and the Seven Dwarves*, *Fantasia*, *The Jungle Book*, and *Dumbo*, to name but a few. In 1955 he also opened his first theme park, Disneyland Park. Disney theme parks now include Disneyland, Walt Disney World, Euro Disney, and Tokyo Disney. Walt's nephew, Roy Disney, led a shareholders' revolt against Disney CEO and chairman Michael Eisner in 2003 and 2004.

As a result, Eisner relinquished his position as CEO in 2004 and stepped down as chairman in 2005. In 2006 Pixar was acquired by Disney for $4.1 billion. The deal made Steve Jobs, Pixar CEO and founder of Apple, the biggest single shareholder of Disney.

....

There are theories that Mickey Mouse is Jewish and that this explained Hitler's antipathy to the big-eared rodent, but there is no evidence to support this, despite the huge sales in Micky Mouse mezzuzahs and menorahs in the early nineties. Mind you, he does have a bossy wife called Minnie . . .

Walt himself was supposedly not too keen on Jews. He reportedly refused to employ Jews in high-level positions at his studio or as actors in his live-action features. Only after his death did a Jewish actor feature prominently in a Disney film (Buddy Hackett in *The Love Bug*, 1969). It might be argued that some of the messages in the films were not exactly conducive to harmonious race relations. Let's face it, *Jungle Book* had the king of swing, Louis Prima, voice the monkey; Dumbo is taunted by black crows who sing da blues, one of which is actually called Jim Crow; and Pinocchio is a boy who wears a skullcap and whose nose grows as a result of lying. I don't know—do I smell a theme?

Ironic, then, that Disney became a worldwide super-brand under a Jew, Michael Eisner (from 1984 to 2005). Southern Baptists and many family organizations attempted boycotts after hearing of Eisner's plans for a Gay Day and after Ellen DeGeneres came out on her eponymous Disney-made show, *Ellen*. The final nail in the coffin occured when he bought Miramax, producer of *Reservoir Dogs* and other ungodly movies and formerly owned by the Weinstein brothers. Some writers have seen this "Judification" of the great institution of Disney as "another instrument in the Jewish campaign to multiculturalize America" (William L. Pierce, "Disney and the Jews: Eisner and His Kind Must Stop Harming Our Children").

Shrek (Yiddish expression of terror) by Dreamworks, released in 2001, would have had ole Walt turning in his grave. Not only did it outgross *Toy Story*, the pioneering Disney/Pixar blockbuster, but it mercilessly sent up Disney's hold on our favorite fairy-tale characters. Disney's response to this alien onslaught? *Pocahontas II*.

Things have picked up since those turbulent days. *The Chronicles of Narnia* launched the first of its seven-movie cycle in December 2005 and grossed $209,119,000 (as of January 3, 2006; source: movieweb.com). The discreetly coded subtext of the film—its subtle Christian allusions—was not lost on the Christian groups that adopted it with a fervor and frenzy last seen during *The Passion of the Christ* marketing campaign. Sadly, Aslan, the Christ-figure lion in *Narnia*, was not mutilated and tortured for two hours to make it a full-fledged Christian movie, but Walden Media (the coproducer whose owner is a Republican Christian devoted to spreading the word of Narnia to every school-child in the nation) was happy to steer Disney back from the abyss with this wholesome, all-around American entertainment.

backlash		impact		j-factor		tzurus		kabbalah		good/not good
6.1	+	7	x	4.25	= 55.67	÷	7	=		7.95

Walt Disney is borderline and therefore NOT GOOD FOR THE JEWS

Easter A Christian festival celebrating the resurrection of Jesus after the crucifixion, Easter marks the end of the forty days of Lent, a period of fasting and penitence that begins on Ash Wednesday and ends on Easter Sunday.

Historically, not the best time of year for Jews. The only show in town is the Passion Play, which tends to depict Jews as treacherous murderers. Traditionally it has been a time for Jews to lie low, as feelings can rise high, especially in parts of Eastern Europe, Venezuela, and the whole of Louisiana. Because Easter falls around Passover time, a further wave of hostility emerged with the Blood Libel—the accusation that Jews were using the blood of Christian children to make matzoh. However, this recipe does not appear in the classic *Book of Jewish Food* by Claudia Roden (Knopf, 1996).

All in all, Easter for Jews is like Christmas for turkeys, or grouse season for, well, grouse. It's a time to pretend you don't exist. Is there any upside to this season? Jews get to buy bulk loads of chocolate Easter eggs at massively reduced prices after the fest is over. In fact, chocoholic Muslims, Hindus, and Jews can be seen working together, picking over the spoils at the "highly discounted" sections of Wal-mart on the day following Easter—and all for Christian-themed candy. Thus Easter can be a time to bring religions and races together.

One could see the coincidence of both Passover and Easter falling at the same time of year as a sign. The Last Supper was, after all, a seder, Jesus is seen as the Paschal Lamb, in most languages Easter is called Pasch ("Easter," unsurprisingly, comes from a pagan goddess), and both festivals close with a huge sigh of relief as the gluttony and close proximity to family members finally comes to an end.

backlash		impact		j-factor		tzurus		kabbalah		good/not good
7	+	6.8	x	3.35	= 46.23	÷	7	=		6.6

Easter is NOT GOOD FOR THE JEWS

eBay Online auction site where people can buy and sell

almost anything from or to anyone anywhere in the world. It was started in 1995 by Pierre Omidyar, and its name is a rather tasteless nod to the efficacy of the Ebola virus. It now claims to be one of the fastest-growing companies of all time. Transactions are based on good faith between the buyer and seller. eBay displays feedback from buyers and sellers to encourage honesty.

Where else can the acquisitive Judologist buy a Harvey Megillah dancing Hasid doll? Mind you, up until May 2001, you could also buy Hitler's pencil case and nasal trimmer, so free markets do have their downsides. eBay did cave in to pressure from the Anti-Defamation League over making profits from Nazi memorabilia and now bans material associated with murders committed in the past one hundred years—except stamps, coins, World War II movies, and so on, so you can still buy *Schindler's List*.

One can still buy some great items of anti-Semitic interest. Hundreds of copies of the *Protocols of the Elders of Zion, Mein Kampf*, and other good old-fashioned race-hate products can be snapped up at a bargain. Strangely for a dot-com business, the founder of this celebration of free enterprise is neither Jewish (jewwatch.com better change its "educational Web site") nor American-born, but French Iranian. Mr. Omidyar has used his fortune in a heimische way, though, and set up charitable foundations with his wife that pour millions into public projects.

But what to do if your auction date is set for Shabbos or, even worse, Rosh Hashanah? As everybody knows, the last moments of an eBay auction matter the most. Could this be a coded anti-Semitic way of excluding Jews from top products? Imagine the sheer vindictiveness of a deadline of Kol Nidre night on the eve of Yom Kippur for, say, the complete *Seinfeld* backlist, or worse, a tallis in pristine condition worn by the Lubavitcher Rebbe? Torture.

backlash	impact	j-factor	tzurus	kabbalah	good/not good
4.5	+ 6.45	x 4.1	= 44.65	÷ 7	= 6.41

eBay is NOT GOOD FOR THE JEWS

Eurovision Song Contest Inspired by the popular Italian San Remo Festival, the Eurovision Song Contest (ESC) was first held in Lugano, Switzerland, in 1956 and was billed as "The Eurovision Grand Prix." The winner was chosen by a jury consisting of two delegates from each country participating in the contest. Though widely ridiculed for the poor quality of performances and anachronistic national costumes, it is hugely popular in Europe, the Middle East, and Africa and is a mainstay of light-entertainment live broadcasting. Conventionally, the host nation is determined by the winner of the previous year's contest. Many international artists have competed in the ESC. These include Celine Dion, Olivia Newton-John, and ABBA.

....

Jews everywhere take serious note of this competition, not necessarily because of their appreciation of the art of the pop song but because it provides a good gauge of international feelings toward the Jews.

The elaborate voting system involves each nation assigning points to its favorite ten entries. Until recently, votes were decided by small juries in each country; now national telephone polls are held during the live broadcast in order to determine point assignment. Countries are not allowed to vote for themselves.

Hence the Jewish obsession with this competition. Ever since Israel joined the competition in 1973, oohs and aahs and I told you sos can be heard in households throughout Europe when Lithuania, Austria, or Poland cast their negative votes for Israel. Other countries suffer too. The United Kingdom's 2003 act, Jemini, did not receive a single point from any European country, which was interpreted as an expression of anger about the British involvement in the war in Iraq. Cyprus and Greece always give each other maximum points regardless of the dreck offered up. They never vote for Turkey.

That Israel is part of Europe might be news to most people, but since Israeli acts have won three times, we should let the matter drop. These Jewish heroes were transvestite and gay icon Dana International (1998); Alpha Beta (1978); and Milk and Honey (geddit?) (1979).

Some might argue that the mighty Israel, feared in the Middle East, might not be best represented by a man who wears dresses and a group with terrible perms. However, to be invited to any party these days is a metziah.

backlash		impact		j-factor		tzurus		kabbalah		good/not good
5.45	+	5.56	x	5.45	=	60	÷	7	=	8.57

The Eurovision Song Contest is GOOD FOR THE JEWS

Fox News Channel Owned by Rupert Murdoch's News International Corporation and available to 85 million subscribers in the United States. Launched in 1996, it was set up to rival CNN and soon began taking its market share of audience. Murdoch, known for his opposition to what he believed was a liberal agenda in U.S. media, was determined to take an alternative editorial stance on his network. Initially shut out of the New York market by TimeWarner's CNN parent company, Fox News was made available there in 1997 and on the rest of TimeWarner's vast cable network in 2001.

Fox CEO Roger Ailes was a former strategist for Nixon and Reagan, so balanced reporting is his watchword. Fox News saw its profits double during the Iraq War, and some say this is due to its patriotic (i.e., prowar) coverage. At the height of the conflict, it had 3.3 million viewers daily.

One of Fox News's many slogans is "Fair and Balanced." An example of this approach, according to bangitout.com, came in the form of a report from Jerusalem filed by the intrepid reporter Geraldo Rivera. When asked by Greta Van Susteren what the mood was like in downtown Jerusalem, he responded, "People are not hopeful, Greta. Hope is not here. There is no hope." He went on to describe deserted streets and empty cafés, but his balance began to waver when he proclaimed that the sky was devoid of hope, as well. "No, not in the sky, either. No hope in the sky. I looked and it is not there." Perhaps some reporters at Fox double as meteorologists? He ended his sober report with "Life is not the same. Here in Israel. Here. In. Israel. This has been Geraldo Rivera, reporting live and trying not to cry." Fairly balanced reporting at its best.

The challenge might be for the Judologist to find anything *bad* for the Jews in Fox News. Famously, it dropped the term "suicide bomber" and replaced it, upon request of Ari Fleischer, President Bush's press secretary, with "homicide bomber." Fairness and Accuracy in Reporting (FAIR) released a report titled *The Most Biased Name in News: Fox News Channel's Extraordinary Right-Wing Tilt*.

Of course, Fox is not just a fanatical right-wing mouthpiece for the Bush administration. It is much more extreme than that.

However, to be "fair and balanced," one should recognize Roger Ailes's very proud scoop on Bush's hidden drunk-driving offense before the 2000 presidential election. This, according to Karl Rove, "cost Bush the popular vote." Does he mean that Bush won the "unpopular vote"?

Just so Jews don't feel too comfortable with Fox News's attitudes, Bill O'Reilly, the channel's most obvious exponent of "We Report, You Decide" values, said about Christmas:

> You have a predominantly Christian nation. You have a federal holiday based on the philosopher Jesus. And you don't wanna hear about it? Come on—if you are really offended, you gotta go to Israel then. I mean because we live in a country founded on Judeo—and that's your guys'—Christian, that's my guys', philosophy. But overwhelmingly, America is Christian. And the holiday is a federal holiday honoring the philosopher Jesus.

How Fox News would have covered the following news stories had it been around two thousand years ago . . .

Billionaire's Twin Betrayal

Brotherly love seemed to be in short supply in Canaan this evening when our Fox News correspondent Frank Ramos caught up with a developing story that has rocked the small town of Elon:

A sting operation, more commonly seen practiced in downtown Little Moab, is alleged to have occurred in the early hours of Sunday morning.

Esau, thirty-four, is heir to the Isaac Forefather billion-shekel fortune. Although a twin, he is older than his brother Jacob Isaacson and therefore expected to receive his birthright and his father's blessing, both of which are compulsory under the new heredity laws.

That was until Jacob, sensationally, dressed in his brother's clothes, in order to trick his ailing father into giving him his brother's rightful blessing. Allegations of blackmail have been made by Esau after papers were submitted to the town hall transferring his birthright to Jacob one year prior to today's shocking events. "Technically, there is nothing we can do," the DA of Canaan County confirms. "Unless the young man returns the birthright on his own volition, I'm afraid it looks like Esau will have to accept this loophole in the Law."

Jacob has left town and his mother, Rebekka (aged 108), is helping local police with their inquiries. Local reports are coming in of a wandering homeless man who fits Jacob's description, picked up on the road to Luza, but this is yet to be confirmed.

New Legislation Threatens Small Business

Copies of the 613 new regulations introduced since the second publication of the Laws of Moses have sent the markets into free fall, Milton Simkins, our financial correspondent, reports:

The SHMTSE fell by a record 299 points, its steepest one-day decline since the Israelites left Egypt. Laws that will go into effect April next year are set to revolutionize the meat, fish, and poultry sectors as well as completely overhaul the existing regulations governing the textile and fashion industries.

"I have to slaughter the animals in totally different ways now," Shlomo Anov, the spokesperson for the Abbatoir Union, said. "New knives, new salting procedures, new everything. These statutes will spell the end to small corner shops."

"It simply doesn't make sense," Abe Simcha of the Natural Wool Association said. "I am now not allowed to mix wool with cotton, and there are pages and pages of nonsensical guidelines which give no rhyme or reason to the manufacturer. This will be a disaster."

A government spokesman was unavailable for comment.

backlash		impact		j-factor		tzurus		kabbalah		good/not good
6.4	+	6.4	x	6.4	= 81.92	÷	7		=	11.7

Fox News Channel is GOOD FOR THE JEWS

***Godfather* Trilogy, the**   Three films about a fictitious Italian Mafia family. The first one, based on Mario Puzo's 1969 novel *The Godfather* and bearing the same title, was released in 1972. It spawned two sequels: *The Godfather Part II* (1974) and *The Godfather Part III* (1990). All three were directed by Francis Ford Coppola.

"The Godfather" (in Italian, *il Padrino*) is a term used to identify the boss of a Mafia clan, the eldest or the most representative member of a family. Don Vito's surname, Corleone, recalls the town of Corleone, Sicily.

The story of an Italian family and its assimilation within corporate America bears no obvious nor direct relevance to the

Jews. It has a low Jew count, but significantly, in *Godfather II*, Michael Corleone betrays Hyman Roth, an overtly Jewish character, when the young Godfather attempts to expand into Cuba from Florida. Aside from the wheezing, emphysemic portrayal of this powerful Jew, it cannot be said that this is either a positive or negative depiction of the Jews. The other Jewish character—who's never referred to as Jewish directly—is Moe Greene (the Bugsy Segal character). In his novel *The Godfather: The Lost Years*, Mark Winegardner introduces Don Forlenza, whose nickname, the "Jewish Don," arises because he surrounds himself with Jewish associates.

Although many mobsters were Jewish, the most successful movie of the 1970s deflected attention from the Jews to the Italians, and subsequent representations in mass culture, such as *The Sopranos*, *Goodfellas*, and *Analyze This*, have all put the blame for the scourge of organized crime firmly on the shoulders of the Italians. Otherwise we might well have been subjected to series titled *The Schneiders*, *Machers*, and *Analysis/Shmanalysis*.

backlash	impact	j-factor	tzurus	kabbalah	good/not good
5	+ 6.15	x 5.4	= 60.2	÷ 7	= 8.6

The Godfather Trilogy is GOOD FOR THE JEWS

Google Internet search engine founded in 1998 by Sergey Brin and Larry Page at Stanford University.

Initially, Google got ten thousand queries per day, compared with 200 million per day currently. The name Google is a play on the word *googol*, the number represented by 1 followed by one hundred zeros.

. . . .

Both Sergey and Larry, the cofounders of Google, are Jewish, a fact which will either fuel conspiracy theories or make them the most eligible "nice Jewish boys" on the planet. Larry seems to have put the eek into geek as he made a working printer out of LEGO. Yes, *LEGO*.

Google lists three to four thousand hate sites worldwide, and recent controversy over jewwatch.com proves that having Jewish founders does not stop anti-Semitism on the Web. More worrying, though, is the recent fad of self-diagnosis, and Googling your health symptoms has been proven to cause anxiety and trauma. This is clearly a problem for the Jews. Don't Be Evil is a lovely company motto (disconcertingly, an anagram of Bend to Live—something the company managed to do with its ethics when it came to censoring sites for the Chinese government in 2006), but let's face it, with this much money in such young hands, "evil is whatever Sergey says is evil" (Eric Schmidt, Google chief executive). Besides, moral statements bear little weight when a Googler is free to make a bomb, construct chemical weapons, and learn how to lynch local ethnic minorities, all at the stroke of a keyboard.

World Timeline
(Part II–AD 1 to AD 1066)

World

AD 1–AD 249	AD 250–AD 499	AD 500–AD 800	AD 500–AD 800
Gospels are written	Constantine the Great legalizes Christianity (313)	King Arthur legend	Pope Gregory creates "God bless you" as the correct response to a sneeze
Goths invade Asia Minor	Attila the Hun invades Roman provinces (433)	Mohammed founds Islam	
Romans persecute Christians	The Vandals sack Rome (455)	Plague wipes out half of Europe	

Jewish

AD 1–AD 249	AD 250–AD 499	AD 500–AD 800	AD 600
Luke outsells Leviticus	Lionkeeping goes underground	*Camelot* opens on Broadway	"Geh, gesundheit" is the street version
First sign of German trouble	Jews ain't got no quarrel with Asians	I'm not saying anything	
Jews keep their heads down	You thought Romans were bad	The other half survives	

AD 500–AD 800	AD 850–AD 900	AD 1066
Arabs conquer Jerusalem	Alfred the Great becomes king of Britain (871)	Norman Conquest of Britain
Russian nation founded by Vikings with capital at Novgorod (855–879)		
Muslim invaders destroy Alexandria Library		
Dome of Rock built		

AD 630–AD 700	AD 850–AD 900	AD 1066
Time to sell up again	Who cares?	French move in
First shtetl prepared		
Massive relief to overdue borrowers		
Ariel Sharon makes first visit		

However, without Google, this book and many others of its ilk would simply not have been written.

The Judological Institute of Spiritual Mathematics (JISM) and Google began talks in 2006 to launch a Jew-only search engine called Joogle, the first all-encompassing directory which filters out all irrelevant information (anything non-Jewish) for the Judologist. So far this has stalled due to a lack of interest from Google.

backlash	impact	j-factor	tzurus	kabbalah	good/not good
6.8 +	6.9 x	7 =	95.9 ÷	7 =	13.7

Google is GOOD FOR THE JEWS

Guilt Culpability for a crime is the most accepted definition of this word. It also denotes remorseful awareness of having done something wrong, or self-reproach for supposed inadequacy or wrongdoing.

If you are one of the Chosen People, of course you are going to feel guilty every day of your life about every single aspect of it. After all, you weren't *chosen* to do badly at school, you weren't *chosen* for being unable to finish those gedempte meatballs lovingly cooked by your mother, you weren't *chosen* for your love of being spanked by a Croat animal trainer on Motze Shabbos, and so on. When standards are high, not reaching them can be a cause of guilt.

What happens to the Jew who feels no guilt? Take away the neuroses and remorse for every act performed daily—what are you left with? A non-Jew.

Leviticus had the right idea. Pages and pages of descriptions of how to beat a goat, skin a cat, and generally torture the animal world to purge yourself of guilt. Now, the Jews don't have scapegoats anymore; every malevolent thought is internalized. Mix this with a strong dose of history, and you have Jewish guilt.

Guilt expresses itself in countless ways. From the heavy-handed—"if you don't finish your latkes, Benjamin, your mother and grandmother will drop dead"—to the more subtle approach exemplified by this story:

During a break in the secret negotiations at Camp David between Israel and Egypt in 1978, Zbigniew Brzezinski, national security adviser to President Jimmy Carter, invited Prime Minister Menachem Begin to play a friendly game of chess with him.

Before Mr. Brzezinski was allowed to make his first move, Premier Begin dramatically seized his hand in midair and said very quietly, "Dr. Brzezinski, do you know when I played my last game of chess?" "No," the adviser quivered. "September 1940, when the NKVD broke into my hiding place in Vilna to arrest me." Shortly afterward, Mrs. Begin passed. "Oh, the two of you are playing chess," she says. "You know, Mr. Brzezinski, Menachem just loves to play. He plays all the time." (source: *The Fifty Years War: Israel and the Arabs*, BBC, Norma Percy)

Without guilt, would peace ever be struck?

backlash	impact	j-factor	tzurus	kabbalah	good/not good
5.25	+ 5.87	x 7	= 77.84	÷ 7	= 11.12

Guilt is GOOD FOR THE JEWS

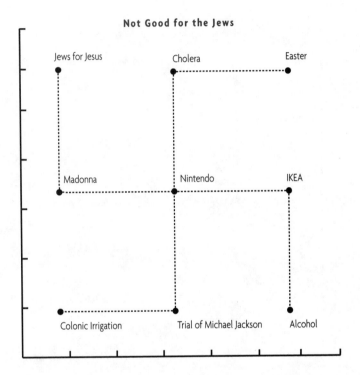

Not Good for the Jews

Note to Judologists: A random sample of entries has been plotted on these two graphs. The pattern of dashed lines is purely coincidental.

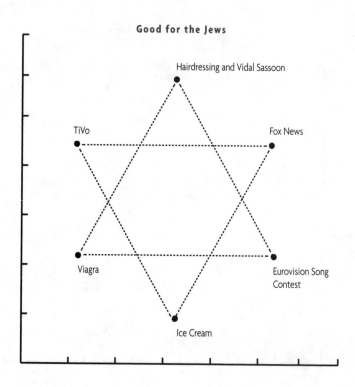

Good for the Jews

- Hairdressing and Vidal Sassoon
- TiVo
- Fox News
- Viagra
- Eurovision Song Contest
- Ice Cream

Hairdressing and Vidal Sassoon A world famous hairdresser and entrepreneur born in London on January 17, 1928, Sassoon rose from humble beginnings to become the father of modern hairdressing. He is the inventor of the bob, the five-point cut, and geometric hairdos perfected during London's swinging sixties. He gave his name to numerous hair products and set up styling academies throughout the United Kingdom and United States. In 1982, he established the Vidal Sassoon International Center for the Study of Antisemitism. The center "engages in research on antisemitism throughout the ages, focusing on relations between Jews and non-Jews, particularly in situations of tension and crisis."

Is hairdressing really a profession for a nice Jewish boy? The most famous proponent of this noble art must be Vidal Sassoon. Though famous for his "Nancy Kwan" cut, he was no nancy boy. Sassoon might have curled and créped by day, but by night he was rumored to have been part of a postwar Jewish vigilante group called the 43 Group that hunted out escaped Nazis. In 1948 he left for Israel to help fight in the War of Independence (May 1948). Perhaps his finest moment, though, came when he represented the Jewish people (actually Los Angeles, the host city) as the official hair stylist at the '84 Olympics, disproving the vicious stereotype that Jews are no good at sporting events.

However, controversy arises when we look at Mr. Sassoon's legacy as Hairdresser to the Nation. Young Jewesses everywhere were influenced by him to forego their heimische curls and adopt his geometric cuts and straight hair. The Twiggy and Mia Farrow looks plunged Jewish identity into crisis and put a generation of Jewish princesses into therapy for years to come.

The Vidal Sassoon International Center for the Study of Anti-semitism spawned many other sober institutions of learning such as the L'Oréal Because I'm Worth It Research Laboratory for International Peace Studies in Vermont and most famously, the Head and Shoulders Center of Islamic Revolution, based in Seattle.

backlash		impact		j-factor		tzurus		kabbalah		good/not good
4.5	+	4.0	x	7	= 59.5	÷	7		=	8.5

Hairdressing and Vidal Sassoon are GOOD FOR THE JEWS

Happiness The state of feeling, showing, or causing pleasure or satisfaction. A sense of well-being characterized by emotions ranging from contentment to intense joy.

The pursuit of happiness is enshrined as a basic right in the U.S. Declaration of Independence, but for Jews who have experienced so much unhappiness throughout history, is it any surprise that it is not high on the agenda of realistic goals? The consensus among psychologists is that negative emotions are fundamental to the human condition, and the brain works by looking for what's wrong—a response programmed from traumas that go back to the Ice Age. In other words, misery was a state of being that existed before the Jews. Hence the Jews do not have a monopoly on discontent—merely a major stake.

"Man hands on misery to man," "Hell is other people," "I never knew what happiness really was until I got married. And then it was too late." These famous quotations are strangely not from Jews but from, respectively, Brit poet Philip Larkin, French philosopher Jean-Paul Sartre (non-Jews), and a book of bad jokes. Misery is not a Jewish phenomenon.

Unhappiness is easier to quantify and market than contentment. Psychologists have always preferred the neurotic, the hysteric, and the depressed to the happy clappy.

However, a Jewish professor of psychology named Martin Seligman, in his best-selling book *Authentic Happiness*, scientifically explains what happiness is and how to achieve it. If this works, quite frankly, it could spell disaster for Jewish identity forever and put a lot of half-decent Jewish comedians out of business.

Seligman maintains you can train your brain to counter the negative forces. He hates Freud, who, he believes, harps on the past and therefore makes you passive about your future. Seligman's formula for happiness includes, among other things, writing down three things that went well every day for a week; identifying your strengths and using one of them in a new and different way every day for a week; writing a letter to someone you're grateful to but have never thanked and going to read it out loud to them.

No wonder we're all so miserable. The stress of finding something good that has happened today would be enough to finish most Jews off.

backlash   impact   j-factor   tzurus   kabbalah   good/not good
3.06   +   5.7   x   1.6   =   14   ÷   7   =   2

Happiness is NOT GOOD FOR THE JEWS

Ice Cream A frozen dessert made from dairy products, flavorings, and sweeteners. A cold, puddinglike form of ice cream first appeared in Persia in 400 BC. In the thirteenth century the Venetian traveler Marco Polo supposedly saw ice cream being made on his trip to China and brought the recipe home with him on his return to Italy. From there, Catherine de' Medici's Italian chefs are said to have carried the recipe to France when she went there in 1533 to marry the duc d'Orléans. (source: wikipedia.org)

The Jews cannot be said to have invented ice cream, but the following founders of Forbes 500 companies must take credit for its mass popularity: Rose and Reuben Mattus (Häagen-Dazs),

Ben Cohen and Jerry Greenfield (Ben & Jerry), Burton Baskin and Irving Robbins (Baskin-Robbins), Charles Lubin (Sara Lee).

King Solomon the Wise is said to have enjoyed iced drinks during harvesttime, and he was pretty clever.

backlash		impact		j-factor		tzurus		kabbalah		good/not good
4.23	+	6.89	x	5.29	=	58.8	÷	7	=	8.4

Ice cream is GOOD FOR THE JEWS

IKEA Swedish furniture company created by Ingvar Kamprad in a southern Swedish backwater in 1943. It started as a small business selling matches before diversifying into pencils. Furniture was introduced in 1953. It now has 225 stores in 33 different countries worldwide with a turnover of 14.5 billion euros. It aims to "offer a wide range of home furnishings with good design and function at prices so low that as many people as possible will be able to afford them. And still have money left!" (IKEA.com) In some countries, the demand for its products is so high that riots have been known to break out when a new store opens, like the one in Edmonton, London, in February 2005 at midnight, when over six thousand customers fought to get in, many sustaining injuries as a result.

It is also a phenomenon in Israel, where, in 2001,

IKEA opened one of its biggest stores in the Middle East (at 23,000 square feet) in Netanya.

....

What is this mishegoss with do-it-yourself furniture? Cheap it may be, but that is no reason to build it yourself. Whatever happened to the old Jewish maxim "I'll get a man in"? Jews who are used to building their own sukkahs (tabernacles) might have a leaning toward these products (see SnapSukkah, the do-it-yourself sukkah), but can IKEA be Good for the Jews?

IKEA assembly can be a symbol of Jewish learning, according to one rabbi. "They always tell you not to tighten the bolts," explains Tzvi Freeman of the Chabad organization, "until the whole thing's been put together." So it is with Jewish learning: Don't expect to know everything until you have learned all the bits and pieces. This, of course, could be just another spurious argument woven by rabbis to get Jews to attend synagogue more.

That aside, it is hard to argue that IKEA is a spiritual experience or one that has been tailored to Jewish needs. Perhaps given IKEA's omnipresence, subliminal messaging might be its more sinister raison d'être. After all, with the circulation of its catalog outstripping that of the Bible (Christian Bibles printed in 2003: 53 million; IKEA catalogs printed in 2003: 115 million), could there be a subconscious agenda being transmitted to us via this vast distribution network? A code, perhaps? Is there any Kabbalistic significance to products with names like Bubbla picture holder, Bygel kitchen range, Benjamin stool, and Alikvot lamp?

As anyone who has visited an IKEA superstore knows, there is only one direction of traffic allowed, and no purchases can be made until the hapless visitor seeking out his plug or one lightbulb has reached the checkout at the end of the path through the store. Such power is given over willingly, but to whom? Well, it was rumored that the founder, Ingvar Kamprad, was once a Nazi, though this charge was subsequently downgraded to mere fascist, which has been massaged to mean "attending one or two lectures by a minor right-winger called Per Engdahl in Malmö, Sweden, in the fifties." However, in December 1995, Kamprad publicly repented for his flirtation with fascism, and his company reportedly paid a sum of reparations to the Anti-Defamation League.

backlash		impact		j-factor		tzurus		kabbalah		good/not good
5.03	+	6.67	x	2.2	= 25.74	÷		7	=	3.68

IKEA is NOT GOOD FOR THE JEWS

Jews* Who Would Be Good to Marry

(Eligibility ratings are out of seven, naturally, with 7 being optimum desirability and 1 being its opposite.)

The Girls

Scarlett Johansson (born November 22, 1984, in New York) American star of *Girl with a Pearl Earring*, *Lost in Translation*, and *Matchpoint*. Don't be misled by her Danish father; look to her mother, Melanie Sloan, for the J-Factor. As if things could not get better, she faced off against Tom Cruise on Scientology and was dropped from *Mission Impossible III* as a result.
Judological eligibility rating: 7

---

*Defined as having at least one Jewish parent or grandparent. Subject may not even know he or she is Jewish.

Neve Adrianne Campbell (born October 3, 1973, in Guelph, Ontario) She moved from teen actress in the TV show *Party of Five* to leading role in *Scream*. Known for her no-nudity clauses, so possibly good for frum Jews. However she does identify herself now as a Catholic, so might not be ideal for baale teshuva.

Judological eligibility rating: 4.5

Sophie Okonedo (born Janury 1, 1969, in London) Oscar-nominated star of *Hotel Rwanda*. When asked why she shunned all the glamorous Hollywood parties she's been invited to, she replied that she couldn't get a good baby-sitter. Heimische.

Judological eligibility rating: 3.5

Winona Ryder (born Winona Laura Horowitz, October 29, 1971, in Winona, Minnesota) As famous for her roles in *Alien: Resurrection*, *Heathers*, and *The Crucible* as she is for shoplifting and having numerous boyfriends. Trouble with a capital *T*.

Judological eligibility rating: 2.5

Monica Samille Lewinsky (born July 23, 1973, in San Francisco) Her fame revolves around a blue dress with semen stains and a cigar that went into the wrong orifice. Nothing wrong with that.

Judological eligibility rating: 7

The Boys

David Blaine (born David Blaine White, April 4, 1973, in Brooklyn, New York) He would be a strange date as he is used to locking himself in ice for days at a time, starving himself above the Thames for several weeks, and standing on very tall pillars for extraordinary lengths of time. Still, he is clearly the kind of guy who sticks around.
Judological eligibility rating: 4.25

Harvey Weinstein (born March 19, 1952, in Queens, New York) If you are in search of a big personality in a big frame, look no further. Not for the sensitive, as he is known for his huge temper, undiminished by his crash dieting, and his, shall we say, "focus." Hugely successful and must be applauded for naming his company Miramax after his mom and pa, Miriam and Max. Nice Jewish boy.
Judological eligibility rating: 4

Sergey Mihailovich Brin (born August 21, 1973 in Moscow) Cofounder of Google, has an estimated wealth of $11 billion, which makes him very eligible. But before any Jewish female readers feel the need to call him up for a date, be warned that small talk with Sergey might well involve phrases like "gagillions" and "entangled nuclear spins."
Judological eligibility rating: 5.5

Boris Becker (born November 22, 1967, in Leiman, Germany) One of the great tennis players, he has a penchant for the ladies. Born on the same day (different year) as Scarlett Johansson, so that sorts out his pickup line. One tip: If he asks you to go in to the broom closet at the restaurant on your first date, *don't go*. Last time he did this at Nobu in London, his five-minute exchange of fluids resulted in a little Becker and a huge child maintenance bill. On the other hand, if you date Boris, go straight to the broom closet.

Judological eligibility rating: 6

Joaquin Rafael Phoenix (born October 28, 1974, in San Juan, Puerto Rico). Also known as Leaf, so clearly suitable for the outdoor type of girl. Famous for his roles in *Gladiator* and *Walk the Line*. Although he has a Jewish-born mother, his parents weren't exactly Shomer Shabbos, as they belonged to the Children of God. So if you are relaxed about which family to go to on Rosh Hashanah, this guy is for you.

Judological eligibility rating: 3.5

Jeans Jeans were invented in Genoa, Italy, when that city was an independent republic and a naval power. The first denim came from Nîmes, France, hence the name denim (de Nîmes). Levi Strauss came to San Francisco in 1853 and opened a dry-goods business. One of his many customers was a tailor named Jacob Davis who hit upon the idea of improving the durability of work trousers by putting metal rivets at the points of strain, such as on the pocket corners and at the base of the button fly. Jacob wrote to Levi to suggest that the two men hold the patent together. Originally worn by miners, farmers, and cowboys, Levi's are now worn by people in all walks of life. Since Levi Strauss's time, pure cotton fabrics have given way to cotton mixed with spandex to provide stretch.

Though clearly designed and marketed by Jews, jeans are still fundamentally a non-Jewish garment. No self-respecting Jew wears spandex material, which accentuates the genitalia[*], when comfortable cotton and wool trousers—proper schmattes—are available.

Having said that, some notable Jews have made money and reputations playing with this synthetic nonsense. These include:

Calvin Klein
Donna Karan
Isaac Mizrahi
Ralph Lauren
Marc Jacobs
Nicole Farhi

Schlemiel enough to pay these prices? You must be Good for the Jews. Jewish tailors have always had a good living as long as they target non-Jews as their primary market. There is an old joke in the rag trade which goes like this: A Gentile goes into a clothing store and says, "This is a very fine jacket. How much is it?" The salesman says, "It's five hundred dollars." The Gentile says, "OK, I'll take it."

[*]See *Kalooki Nights* by Howard Jacobson (Cape, 2006). "It is considered inappropriate by Jews to show strangers of either sex the outline of your glans penis."

backlash		impact		j-factor		tzurus		kabbalah		good/not good
3	+	6.25	x	7	= 64.75	÷	7	=		9.25

Jeans are GOOD FOR THE JEWS

. . . .

Jews for Jesus Moishe Rosen officially founded Jews for Jesus in September of 1973 in San Francisco, although its headquarters boast a start date of AD 32. Today, Jews for Jesus is an international ministry with a staff of 214 spread out over eleven countries and twenty cities. Its Web site states, "We believe that Jesus the Messiah was eternally pre-existent and is co-equal with God the Father; that He took on Himself the nature of man through the virgin birth." In other words, these Jews believe that Jesus was the Messiah and that their duty is to spread this message. The group has been branded as a cult and the Web site exjewsforjesus.org, warns of certain suspect practices such as "pain training" and "shunning" of former members.

. . . .

Touchy subject this.

Are Jews for Jesus trying to have it all? One day it's "an eye for an eye," next it's "turn the other cheek." Makes for a messy face.

On the other hand, Jesus was Jewish, so why be ashamed

of it? After all, Jews have been blamed for his death by everyone from Matthew to Mel Gibson, so why not take credit for the upside of this story? And his mother was a virgin—what Jewish father could ask for more of his daughter?

If we take away the thorny issue of the crucifixion and the fact the Jews believe the Messiah hasn't come yet, Jews for Jesus has a lot in common with some Hasidic sects. Both enjoy lots of religious holidays (J4J's get double the amount!) and both believe the Messiah has come already; followers of the Lubavitcher Rebbe, Menachem Schneerson, published huge newspaper ads and rented billboards to tell everyone that their rabbi was the promised Messiah—hesitating only when he died on June 12, 1994, at age ninety-two, and wasn't, er, actually, the Messiah. Well, not yet, anyway.

backlash		*impact*		*j-factor*		*tzurus*		*kabbalah*		*good/not good*
7	+	3.1	x	3.5	= 35.35 ÷	7	=			5.05

Jews for Jesus are NOT GOOD FOR THE JEWS

Jew or False?

ere's a little breather game for the amateur Judologist. Which of the following has one or more Jewish parent/grandparent?

1. Harrison Ford (actor)
2. Sean Penn (actor)
3. Ron Jeremy (porn star)
4. Harvey Keitel (actor)
5. Michael Landon (actor)
6. Ralph Lauren (designer)
7. Nostradamus (fortune-teller)
8. Nina Hartley (porn star)
9. Danielle Steele (best-selling author)
10. Walter Mosley (crime writer)
11. Gwyneth Paltrow (actress)
12. Jennifer Connelly (actress)
13. Adrien Brody (actor)
14. Lindsey Vuolo (porn star)

Answer: Jews! They are all Jews!

Jews Who Are Good
for the Jews

Alan Greenspan (born March 6, 1926, in New York) Chairman of the Federal Reserve from 1987 to 2006. This very good sax player happened to know a thing or two about interest rates. He straddled the Reagan, Bush, Clinton, and Bush Jr. administrations like a colossus. His word was law. During his eighteen-year reign, he weathered Black Monday in October 1987, saw the creation of 27 million new jobs and a rise in spending per capita of 44 percent, and experienced only two recessions. He ditched the Milton Friedman doctrine in 1996, and several countries around the world followed suit, copying his low-interest-rate fetish. Greenspan retired in 2006, picking up a healthy $8.5 million for his memoirs from Penguin. A kosher deal. Succeeded by Benjamin Shalom Bernanke. The markets breathed an anti-Semitic sigh of relief that another Jew won't give away the family jewels.

Mark Spitz (born February 10, 1950, in Modesto, California) In his early years, he didn't quite live up to the name of his hometown—he predicted he would win six gold medals in the 1968 Olympics. In fact he won two. In the 1972 Munich games he won seven golds in the butterfly and freestyle events, so best not tease him too much. A sporting legend. Two words not used about Jews since David slew Goliath.

Judith Resnick (born April 5, 1949, in Akron, Ohio; died January 28, 1986) This granddaughter of a rabbi became the first Jewish astronaut and second woman ever to travel in space. After her trip on the Space Shuttle *Discovery* in 1984, she was picked for the fateful *Challenger* expedition that resulted in the death of all seven crew members. She is also the only Jewish person ever to have a crater on Venus named after her.

Fiorello La Guardia (born December 11, 1882, in New York; died September 20, 1947) The American politician famous for being the only Jew to have a U.S. airport named after him. Certain pleasure must be had from the thought that some of the world's most ferociously anti-Semitic terrorists have flown into this Jewish airport. After World War I, he served several terms in Congress, where he opposed Prohibition and supported child labor laws as well as votes for women. He served as mayor of New York from 1933 to 1945, where he ended years of corruption, cleared the slums, and created low-cost housing.

Jews Who Are Not Good for the Jews

Bugsy Siegel (born Benjamin Siegelbaum, February 28, 1906, in Brooklyn, New York; died June 20, 1947) Murder Inc.'s representative in the sunshine state. Famed for seeing the huge potential of Las Vegas as a gambling mecca; through gentle persuasion (extortion) and clever finance deals (exortion), Bugsy built the Flamingo Hotel, the center of world gambling. Unfortunately, he skimmed too much off the top (you just can't get good accountants in Nevada) and was bumped off. Pioneer or playboy?

Bruno Kreisky (born January 22, 1911, in Vienna, Austria; died July 29, 1990) The chancellor of Austria from 1970 to 1983. Yes, you heard right, Austria. A Jew as chancellor of the most anti-Semitic country in Europe must be taken seriously. Not wishing to be seen as too Jewish, he appointed four former Nazis to his cabinet, was very happy to include war criminals in his coalition (Friedrich Peter, far-right leader who was exposed as a member of a troop that murdered thousands of Jews), and was one of the first European leaders to welcome Yasser Arafat. Self-hating or visionary statesman?

Meyer "The Brain" Lansky (born Majer Suchowlinski, July 4, 1902, in Grodno, Poland; died January 15, 1983) This murdering gangster holds a special place in the hearts of Judologists everywhere, as his lifelong motto was "Is it good for Meyer?" Went into business with Lucky Luciano and they formed the National Crime Syndicate, though it was unusual for non-Italians to be allowed entry. Lansky operated in Cuba, Florida, and Vegas on gambling projects, and the character Hyman Roth in *The Godfather Part II* is based on him. Despite fleeing to Israel and "donating" millions to the Zionist cause, he was sent packing in 1972 but acquitted in U.S. court in 1973 for tax evasion. One positive result of his sojourn in the Promised Land was a tightening up of the Law of Return. He was said to have amassed $100 million in profits from drugs, gambling, and prostitution. Enterprising businessman with multicultural links or murdering shyster?

Karma (Sanskrit, from the root *kri*, "to do") A concept central to Eastern religion (Hinduism, Sikhism, Buddhism, and Jainism). It means that the actions a person takes or the thoughts a person has throughout his or her life directly affect what happens to him or her in this life and in subsequent lives. It refers to the cycle of cause and effect. A person who commits good acts has good karma; a person who commits bad acts has bad karma. Karma may not come to fruition in a person's lifetime but may occur in rebirth, so a good person may be reincarnated to a superior life and a bad person may be reincarnated to an inferior life, for example, as an animal.

Deuteronomy 19:21 says: "Life shall go for life, eye for eye, tooth for tooth"—not exactly what the ancient Easterns meant by karma, but a Jewish version nonetheless.

Jews have been drawn to Buddhism since the sixties, and in the San Francisco Bay Area there are many Jewish Buddhist teachers who see a compatibility between notions of suffering and spiritual solace. They also smoke a lot of dope in the Bay Area, so they have plenty of time to sit around saying things like "shit happens."

Jews who have seen the Eastern light are now called JUBUs, and there are many famous JUBUs—Leonard Cohen, Goldie Hawn, Steven Seagal, Allen Ginsberg, and David Ben-Gurion. An old JUBU story tells of how a Jewish mother spent six months trekking up a Nepalese mountain to seek an audience with the holy guru Master Shin-Yeng Lu only to say three words when she finally reached the summit: "Herschel, come home."

Jews and karma have a rocky relationship. After all, who is going to argue that five thousand years of suffering was brought about by things they did when they were small? Mind you, it is quite a challenge to think how gangsters like Bugsy Siegel and Meyer Lansky will be reincarnated. What is in store for villains like Joel Rifkind, Leopold and Loeb, Mickey Cohen, Jack Abramoff, and Jerry Springer? What animal will be honored by bearing Yigal Amir's soul? Or worse, Joan Rivers's? Mind you, it could be said that she has come back again, this time as a mad cow.

backlash	impact	j-factor	tzurus	kabbalah	good/not good
5.9 +	4.5 x	5.1	= 53.04	÷7 =	7.58

Karma is borderline and therefore NOT GOOD FOR THE JEWS

....

K-Y Jelly A water-based personal lubricant produced by Johnson & Johnson, it was created in 1917 and was then known as Jelly Personal Lubricant. No one knows why it is called K-Y Jelly. Some believe it is because it was created in Kentucky (hence KY). It was not available over the counter until 1980. It was first marketed only to doctors for use during pelvic exams of female patients and today is mainly used as a sexual lubricant. It contains no colors or perfumes and is water-soluble. (source: K-Y Web site)

....

The age-old debate as to whether sexual intercourse is better with or without a circumcised penis rages on. There is a strong case to be argued that the friction caused by a circumcised member during intercourse removes the natural lubricants of the female of the species and therefore K-Y Jelly is a necessary aid to fulfilling the mitzvah of pleasuring one's wife.

Lubrication, at first glance, might not seem a particularly edifying topic of discussion for the serious Judologist, but sex is widely discussed in the Torah. In fact, Genesis makes it clear that sex is linked to knowledge—the Hebrew word *yada* means "knowing"; Adam *knew* Eve (an ethereal nudge nudge, wink wink), and they ate from the Tree of Knowledge (geddit?). Sex is serious business. So what's wrong with getting it right?

Wilhelm Reich argued in his book *The Function of the Orgasm* (1927) that failure to reach orgasm can lead to neurosis. Another argument for K-Y in every Jewish household? However, before logging on to gotosextoys.com, remember: Judaism is about fertility rather than eroticism. Medieval Ashkenazis sought an erotic link to the Primary Mover rather than focusing their attention on the baser corporeal experience. Puts the phrase "did the earth move for you?" into historical perspective. It can also explain many young Jewish males' belief that they are God's gift to women.

Warning: Applying K-Y Jelly is a very messy procedure—which can be off-putting for Jewish women who can't bear untidy bedrooms and are used to getting a handyman to do everything for them.

backlash	impact	j-factor	tzurus	kabbalah	good/not good
2	+ 4.45 x	2.4	= 15.48 ÷	7 =	2.21

K-Y Jelly is NOT GOOD FOR THE JEWS

Lawson, Nigella (born January 6, 1960, in London) A cookbook writer, journalist, and television personality. She is the daughter of the former British chancellor of the exchequer, Nigel Lawson, and the late society beauty Vanessa Salmon. Her brother, Dominic Lawson, was the former editor of the *Sunday Telegraph*. She is the author of five best-sellers: *How to Eat* (1999), *Nigella Bites* (2001), *How to Be a Domestic Goddess* (2003), *Feast* (2004), and *Forever Summer* (2005).

Anyone who describes a simple raspberry as "slut-red" is welcome in my house.

Nigella, with her feminized father's name, is perhaps the

ultimate Jewish fantasy figure. To women, she is an intelligent, sensual woman who enjoys her curves. To men, she is an intelligent, sensual women whose curves you want to enjoy.

Nigella's Jewishness is not necessarily central to her cooking. However, she does like to mix and match ethnic dishes. It is not uncommon to see her licking her lips erotically while pummeling gefilte fish into shape. The question on Judologists' minds must be: What effect does this siren of the stove have on the Jewish psyche? Is she the ultimate baleboosteh figure with the tzimmes always simmering at the ready? Or is she the Lilith of the Latkes, ready to pour bread sauce over your vermicelli? Is she Golda from *Fiddler on the Roof* or Sharon Stone from *Basic Instinct*?

Well, she does cook Jewish dishes but has been known to recommend them after serious treyf. For example, her wonderful lokshen pudding, the recipe for which appears in *Feast*, is recommended to follow roast pork loin. Like Moses, she leads you to the Promised Land but won't take you there. She has also been known to say, "Christmas isn't complete if you haven't got a ham as well as a turkey." Boy, does she know how to drive a young Jewish boy mad.

backlash	impact	j-factor	tzurus	kabbalah	good/not good
4.25	+ 5.75	x 6.9	= 69	÷ 7	= 9.85

Nigella Lawson is GOOD FOR THE JEWS

Lawyers Webster's dictionary defines a lawyer as "one whose profession is to conduct lawsuits for clients or to advise as to legal rights and obligations in other matters." Western law can be said to have its origins in the Old Testament when, in approximately 1300 BC, Moses received a list of ten laws directly from God. The first recorded legal ruling came in 1750 BC, when Hammurabi, king of Babylon, developed the oldest existing code of laws.

There are countless jokes made at the expense of lawyers, painting them as liars, cheats, and extortionists. How can you tell when a lawyer is lying? His lips are moving. You're trapped in a room with a tiger, a rattlesnake, and a lawyer. Your gun has only two bullets. What should you do? Shoot the lawyer—*twice*. And so on. Why, then, is the law so attractive to Jewish mothers as a career path for their offspring? Is it Good for the Jews that Jews are prominent in such a maligned profession?

At heart, Judaism is an argument over the law, so why not make a living out of it? In the Bible there are 613 mitzvoth (commandments) and books and books of commentary on these laws in the Mishnah and Gemara, so Jews are trained from an early age to hone their analytical skills. But do they have to keep you on the phone so long?

Lawyers are not all venal. Many Jews have been important figures in the civil rights movement. For every two-bit shyster there is a lawyer like William Kunstler, who fought for Lenny Bruce, Malcolm X, the Native Americans, and many more. It must be noted that the desire for litigation can rebound on even the most noble of lawsuits. For example, lawyers helped in the suit against the Swiss government to reclaim some of the stolen gold of Holocaust survivors. Not to be outdone, there is now a lawsuit from Egyptian lawyers planning to sue "all the Jews of the world" over gold that was allegedly stolen during the biblical exodus of the Israelites from Egypt. Dr. Nabil Hilmi, dean of the faculty of law at the University of Al-Zaqaziq, argues that the Israelites stole jewelry and cooking utensils, fleeing in the middle of the night with all this wealth and not even leaving a thank-you note.

backlash		impact		j-factor		tzurus		kabbalah		good/not good
6.57	+	3.45	x	5.25	=	52.6	÷	7	=	7.51

Lawyers are borderline and therefore NOT GOOD FOR THE JEWS

Lewinsky, Monica Samille (born July 23, 1973, in San Francisco) In 1995 Monica Lewinsky was an intern at the White House. In January 1998 a tape was released of a conversation between Monica and Pentagon employee

Linda Tripp which revealed Lewinsky and President Bill Clinton were conducting an illicit affair. The president was impeached when he was forced to admit the "inappropriate relationship." Lewinsky later started a new career as a handbag designer and is currently studying at the London School of Economics.

"I did not have sexual relations with that woman" were the words spoken by President Clinton to the media at the height of the scandal. Faint echoes of "There will be no whitewash in the White House" made twenty years earlier by President Nixon? Both statements turned out to be sophistry—"no sex" meant "a blow job and playing around with a cigar" and "no whitewash" meant "complete and utter whitewash."

Is Monica a dream intern/employee or a Jewish princess nightmare? The jury is out because some might argue that President Clinton was interested not so much in her Jewish identity as her Jewish mouth. As the following quotes from a Syrian newspaper show, her Jewishness did seem relevant to some people:

> Monica is a Jewess, the lawyers who volunteered to defend her were Jews, Monica's friends who recorded the hot phone conversations between her and President Clinton were Jewesses and the *Washington Post* newspaper which published the affair for the first time is a Jewish newspaper . . . Her goal was to

embarrass President Clinton, to blackmail him and weaken his status before Netanyahu's government.

Tishrin al-Usbu'a, August 24, 1998

Monica will sadly go down on history as the one with the cigar and for this reason her legacy to world Jewry is not wholly positive. Having said that, many Jews are still amazed to hear of a Jewish woman on her knees, even once.

She is also responsible for renaming the Jew's harp (a small lyre-shaped instrument that is placed between the teeth and played by twanging a wire tongue while changing the shape of the mouth cavity) to Monica's harp, which is Good for the Jews.

backlash	impact	j-factor	tzurus	kabbalah	good/not good
5.5 +	5.45 x	7	= 76.65 ÷	7	= 10.95

Monica Lewinsky is GOOD FOR THE JEWS

Writers Who Are Not
Good for the Jews

If you are the type of person who can no longer enjoy Great Works of Literature if you learn negative things about your favorite authors, then please skip this section. All the below are Not Good for the Jews. Their Judological rating is given beneath each entry. Remember, the lower the number, the less Good this writer is for the Jews.

Roald Dahl (1916–1990) Author of *James and the Giant Peach* (1961), *The Twits* (1980), *The BFG* (1982), *Matilda* (1988). Dahl once told a journalist: "There's a trait in the Jewish character that does provoke animosity . . . I mean there is always a reason why anti-anything crops up anywhere; even a stinker like Hitler didn't just pick on them for no reason." This slip of the tongue—for what else could it be?—lost him his knighthood chances and made him even more embittered against the Jews. After all, the

Child Catcher in *Chitty Chitty Bang Bang*, the movie he scripted, was nothing like a stereotype of a Jew—black hat, long black coat, and huge pointy nose. Some Judologists have argued that his most popular oeuvre, *Charlie and the Chocolate Factory*, can be read as a very dark fable—innocent children tricked into a concentration camp complex manned by strange subhumans who take them away one by one—but the Institute would like to distance itself from such a position.

Judological rating: 2.25

Mark Twain (1835–1910) Author of *The Adventures of Huckleberry Finn* (1885), *The Adventures of Tom Sawyer* (1876). Described Jews as "simple, superstitious, disease-tortured creatures" who could only understand a transcendental idea "if it was written on their skins."

Judological rating: 2.75

Ernest Hemingway (1899–1961) Author of *The Sun Also Rises* (1926), *To Have and Have Not* (1937), *For Whom the Bell Tolls* (1940). Often ranted about "kikes" in his letters. This often translated into less-than-flattering "Jew" characters such as Robert Cohn in *The Sun Also Rises* and self-indulgent tirades against Jews in stories such as "Fifty Grand."

Judological rating: 3.25

Charles Dickens (1812–1870) Author of *The Adventures of Oliver Twist* (1838), *David Copperfield* (1850), *Bleak House* (1853). In the first 38 chapters of *Oliver Twist* there are 257 references to "the Jew" against 42 to "Fagin," who is described as "villainous looking and repulsive." Dickens made no secret that Fagin was based on Jews of that period when he claimed "that class of criminal almost invariably was a Jew." However, he did redeem himself with *Our Mutual Friend*, where he portrayed the noble character of Riah, an elderly Jew who looks after young fallen women. In a letter, Dickens said, "There is nothing but good will left between me and a People for whom I have a real regard." Some of my best friends are . . .

Judological rating: 3.75

Kingsley Amis (1922–1995) Author of *Lucky Jim* (1954), *Girl, 20* (1971), *The Old Devils* (1986). An interviewer once asked Amis whether he was anti-Semitic. "Very, very mildly," replied Amis. Pressed to elaborate, he offered this: "Well, when I'm watching the credits roll at the end of a TV program, I say to myself: 'Oh, there's another one.'"

Judological rating: 4.2

Agatha Christie (1890–1976) Author of *The Murder at the Vicarage* (1930), *Murder on the Orient Express* (1934), *Death on the Nile* (1937). In *The Mysterious Mr. Quin*, this lovely description of Jews is included: "men of Hebraic extraction, sallow men with hooked noses, wearing flamboyant jewellery." *Peril at End House* has a character referred to as "the long-nosed Mr. Lazarus," of whom somebody says, "He's a Jew, of course, but a frightfully decent one." The original title of *And Then There Were None* was, of course, "Ten Little Niggers," which might reflect an underlying attitude to people of other races.

Judological rating 3.95

Dorothy Sayers (1893–1957) Creator of Lord Peter Wimsey. In the 1940s, she wrote an essay in *The Future of the Jews* by J. J. Lynx in which she argues that Jews are bad citizens with little or no loyalty to the country they live in.

Judological rating: 4.3

Graham Greene (1904–1991) Author of *Brighton Rock* (1938), *The Third Man* (1950), *The End of the Affair* (1951). "She deserved something better than a man named Furtstein . . . The domed Semitic forehead, the dark eyes over the rather gaudy tie" (*The Confidential Agent*). "How the financial crisis has improved English films! They have lost their tasteless Semitic opulence and are becoming—English" (*The Spectator*, April 7, 1939).

Judological rating: 5

F. Scott Fitzgerald (1896–1940) Author of *The Beautiful and the Damned* (1922), *The Great Gatsby* (1925), *Tender Is the Night* (1934). In *The Great Gatsby*, the narrator encounters Gatsby's friend Meyer Wolfsheim, a shady gambler who "fixed the World Series in 1919." The narrator describes him as "a small, flat-nosed Jew" who "raised his large head and regarded me with two fine growths of hair which luxuriated in either nostril. After a moment I discovered his tiny eyes in the half-darkness." Every description of Wolfsheim that follows refers to his nose: he "covered Gatsby with his expressive nose," "Mr. Wolfsheim's nose flashed at me indignantly," "His nostrils turned to me in an interesting way," "As he turned away his tragic nose was trembling."

Judological rating: 3.75

John Fowles (1926–2005) Author of the *The Collector* (1963), *The Magus* (1965), *The French Lieutenant's Woman* (1969). In his diaries, Fowles describes his publisher Tom Maschler: "Of all the Jews I know he is the most Jewish: the perfect example of the bitter, wandering, cast-out son of Israel." Milton Shulman, the theater critic, was also described in such terms as a man who has "that Canadian Jewish love of being outrageous, a little comical, as talk-monopolizing as Dr. Johnson . . . These people (this state of mind) have far too much power." Shame, I liked *The Magus*.

Judological rating: 4.65

Madonna Louise Ciccone (born August 16, 1958, in Bay City, Michigan) An American singer frequently referred to as the Queen of Pop Music. Many consider Madonna to be one of the most iconic figures of the late twentieth century.

Madonna is the most famous member of the Kabbalah Centre. Madonna adopted a Hebrew name—Esther—but she was born a Catholic, and many Orthodox Jews believe a non-Jew has no place studying Kabbalah. Strictly speaking, it is forbidden for non-Jews, women, and all men under the age of forty to learn Kabbalah. Kabbalah is regarded by some as the highest form of Judaism, and those who practice it need to be extremely spiritual, modest, and wise, surrounding themselves with holiness and purity. Her hit song "Like a Virgin" (1984) is a strong positive signal in this direction, but unfortunately "Hanky Panky" (in the *Dick Tracy* movie, 1990) might well have damaged her case somewhat.

Kabbalah, which means "that which is received," is a name for the arcane works of Jewish mysticism that were first set down in the Middle Ages and collected in thirteenth-century Spain. Its theoretical content is regarded as profound, if esoteric, but its practical applications border on the magical. Even very observant Jews seldom dip in.

The word *Madonna* has seven letters. As we've seen, the number 7 has spiritual significance in Judology. There are seven days of the week, Yom Kippur and Rosh Hashanah occur in the seventh month of the Hebrew calendar, there are seven Laws of Noah, the Torah begins with a verse containing seven words, we sit shiva for seven days when a close relative dies, Moses was the seventh generation after Abraham, God created seven levels of heaven (hence the expression, "I'm in seventh heaven!"), the world has seven continents. Think about it, coincidence?

The other argument is that she kissed a black Jesus surrounded by burning crosses. That is chutzpah.

backlash		*impact*		*j-factor*		*tzurus*		*Kabbalah*		*good/not good*
5.56	+	3.15	x	2.89	= 25.17	÷	7	=		3.59

Madonna is NOT GOOD FOR THE JEWS

Marijuana, or Cannabis A drug produced from the dried leaves and flowers of the hemp plant. It is thought to have medicinal as well as psychoactive effects, and there is evidence that it has been in use since ancient times. Effects vary and include increased appetite, dry mouth, euphoria, paranoia, and short-term memory loss. Marijuana is also called pot, spliff, or ganga.

Pot can increase paranoia which, frankly, is all the Jews need.

There is a hippie side to the Kabbalah which appeals to pot-smoking frumers who wish to connect with the divine energy flow, and many a Hanukkah table has hamantashen hash cakes for the over-bar-mitzvahs.

Theories abound that Jesus used cannabis ointment to help with his healing abilities. The recipe for anointing oil recorded in Exodus (30:23–25) includes *kaneh-bosm*, phonetically similar to "cannabis," and most in the archaeology community agree that hashish has been around for 1,600 years. A reference to *qeneh* in Isaiah 43:24 refers to a "sweet-tasting" plant. I'm really not sure what kind of shit he was taking there, but Isaiah was a trippy guy.

The Bible makes countless references to people getting stoned.

President Nixon should have the final word: "You know," he said to Bob Haldeman, "it's a funny thing, every one of the

World Timeline
(Part III — AD 1095 to AD 1750)

World				
AD 1095–AD 1099	AD 1100–AD 1200	AD 1215	AD 1337–AD 1453	AD 1350–AD 1450
First Crusade	Universities begin	King John signs the Magna Carta	Hundred Years' War	Political chaos in Germany

Jewish				
AD 1095–AD 1099	AD 1100–AD 1200	AD 1215	AD 1337–AD 1453	AD 1350–AD 1450
Here We Go!	Jews begin quest for –ologies	First real estate office opens for business	Sorry, in my book that is 116 years	Now, there's a surprise

AD 1470	AD 1492	AD 1498	AD 1491–AD 1597	AD 1685–AD 1750
William Caxton publishes first book	Columbus sails the ocean blue	Leonardo da Vinci paints *The Last Supper*	King Henry VIII has six wives	J. S. Bach and boom in classical music

AD 1470	AD 1492	AD 1498	AD 1491–AD 1597	AD 1685–AD 1750
First publishers' lunch—nine hours	Columbus was Jewish, you know. Oh, yes, Jews expelled from Spain	Mary Magdalene has twins	Clearly none of them were Jewish or he would have died much earlier	*Bach, Mozart, and Beethoven—The Movie* scheduled. Stallone says "I'll be Mozart," Vin Diesel says "I'll be Beethoven," and Arnie says "I'll be Bach"

bastards that are out for legalizing marijuana is Jewish. What the Christ is the matter with the Jews, Bob? What is the matter with them? I suppose it is because most of them are psychiatrists." (source: *The Washington Post*)

backlash   impact   j-factor   tzurus   kabbalah   good/not good

5.23   +   6.01   x   6   = 67.44   ÷   7   =   9.63

Marijuana, or cannabis is GOOD FOR THE JEWS

Musical, the A play or film whose action and dialogue is interspersed with singing and dancing and where music plays an extended, primary role. *The Beggar's Opera* of 1728 is said to be the first example of musical theater or operetta as opposed to actual opera. The growth in the musical occurred in the first half of the twentieth century with landmark shows such as *Annie Get Your Gun*, *Showboat*, *Carousel*, and *Oklahoma*. From the sixties on, the musical has generated billions of dollars in productions such as *The Sound of Music*, *Fiddler on the Roof*, and *The Phantom of the Opera*.

It is not controversial to say that Jews dominated the writing, composing, and production of the Broadway musical in the first half of the twentieth century. One can see that many Jews, such as Oscar Hammerstein, Jerome Kern, Richard Rodgers, George and Ira Gershwin, Leonard Bernstein, and Stephen Sondheim, influenced how Americans saw their country by using a Jewish perspective on non-Jewish subjects (ever met a Jew in Oklahoma?).

Hardly surprising, then, to discover that the composer of the biggest-selling song ever, "White Christmas," and whose songs appeared in the huge hit movie *Easter Parade* was of course a Jew named Irving Berlin (né Israel Isidore Baline). Perhaps Izzy thought he wouldn't make money on ditties like "Chappy Chanukah" and "Pesach Parade." Mind you, Berlin's early minor success came with the touching song "Yiddle on Your Fiddle" (1909), but he knew it had limited appeal. The crowning glory, though, must be his composition "God Bless America." Let's face it, who else could have written it? A non-Jew? Feh!

Why are Jews good at musical theater? Perhaps, with a history that is nothing to sing about, Jews turn to fantasy and song? Moments of profundity can occur in the American musical, like when Tevye, the milkman in *Fiddler on the Roof*, says, "We are your chosen people. But, once in a while, can't you choose someone else?"

However, musical theater tends to be about very non-Jewish subjects. Judge for yourself with this random sample of Jewish compositions:

> **Showboat** *Love on a Mississippi cruiser featuring a gambler named Gaylord*

Oklahoma The conflict between cowboys and farmhands

On the Town Three sailors in New York looking for a good time with no money. Looking for girls. Enough said

West Side Story Italians and Hispanics battle it out over a Romeo and Juliet *story line*

Brigadoon Invisible Scottish village inhabited by mad people with shaky accents singing to Gene Kelly

The King and I Thai king hires opinionated, fussy woman to look after his family—actually, quite Jewish when you think about it

The show that broke the mold and made the Broadway musical relevant, vibrant, and intellectually rigorous was, of course, *The Producers*. Or, *Springtime for Hitler: A Gay Romp with Adolf and Eva in Berchtesgaden*, as it is known in the play and film. Mel Brooks, the show's creator, often thanked Hitler for his inspiration. In reality, his true inspiration was *A Night at the Opera*, the Marx Brothers film, whose central premise was making money out of a flop, but as Michael Caine once said when reviewing his acting career, "If you are going to steal, steal from the best." Many have been offended by this musical, but comedy is a typical Jewish way of dealing with tragedy, and Mel Brooks argues that jokes at Hitler's expense (à la Chaplin in *The Great Dictator*) are a way of "laughing the Nazis into oblivion."

backlash		impact		j-factor		tzurus		kabbalah		good/not good
4.25	+	6.35	x	6.1	= 64.7	÷	7	=		9.24

The musical is GOOD FOR THE JEWS

Mustache, the A growth of facial hair on the upper lip most often worn by men, though occasionally they also adorn women. Mustaches come in different shapes and sizes, for example, the pencil mustache (Errol Flynn John Waters), the Dalí (as in Salvador), natural, walrus, handlebar, Wild West, Fu Manchu, or imperial.

Can the type of mustache you wear be Good for the Jews? The small box-shaped 'stache was made famous by Adolf Hitler (1889–1945) yet ridiculed in the same era by Charlie Chaplin (1889–1977). The pleasure one derives from defacing a famous politician's visage on a poster by drawing a "Hitler mustache" must also not be underestimated.

Other famous mustache wearers include Joseph Stalin (1879–1953), the Soviet dictator, whose mustache was large and walruslike but well-kempt. As with a modern-day tyrant, Saddam Hussein (1937–), the mustache choice of these brutal megalomaniacs cannot be seen as proof of anti-Semitism. The walrus look was used by Albert Einstein (1879–1955). Although Professor Einstein turned down the job of president of the State of Israel, his mustache was not part of the decision. At least he bothered to grow his own walrus, which is more than can be said of Groucho Marx (1890–1977), who sprayed his on. He did go on to grow one for real in his dotage, but the damage had been done.

Does a beard diminish the power of the mustache? When Saddam Hussein was discovered in a hole after losing the second Gulf War, the world was shocked not so much by his thin, gaunt expression as his unbearable hirsuteness. In fact, he looked like a Sephardic rabbi after Yom Kippur. He continued to sport the beard/mustache combo in captivity and perhaps sealed his fate.

There are countless other world leaders who have affected Jewish life and have unashamedly sported mustaches—Lech Walesa, Marshal Pétain, Golda Meir, to name but a few. Neville Chamberlain (1869–1940), the British prime minister who limited immigration of Jews to Palestine in the 1930s and did a deal with Hitler in 1938, provides a good example of a natural-looking mustache that had dire effects on World Jewry. Perhaps the most famous facial hair in history was that of Esau in the Bible, who was the victim of a double theft from his twin brother—his birthright and father's blessing—and then, as victim of this hostile takeover, was forced to accept the accession of Jacob as Father of the Jewish Nation. Hair does not seem to get you far. Also, he was a ginger.

backlash   impact   j-factor   tzurus   kabbalah   good/not good

$$4 \;+\; 5 \;\times\; 4 \;=\; 36 \;\div\; 7 \;=\; 5.14$$

The mustache is NOT GOOD FOR THE JEWS

Movies That Are Good for the Jews

Tora! Tora! Tora! (1970, dir. Richard Fleischer, Kinji Fukasaku; starring Martin Balsam and Sô Yamamura) One letter away from being a decent movie.

Taking of Pelham One, Two, Three (1974, dir. Joseph Sargent; starring Walther Matthau, Robert Shaw—and Martin Balsam, again) Only mainstream movie in the seventies to have a Jewish detective whose last line is a Yiddish word ("gesundheit"). Martin Balsam is Jewish, too.

Marathon Man (1976, dir. John Schlesinger; starring Dustin Hoffman and Laurence Olivier) Jew as good athlete. Inspiring. Also, for once, the truth about dentists.

The Passion of the Christ (2004, dir. Mel Gibson; starring James Caviezel, Maia Morgenstern, and Monica

Bellucci) Well, it can't get worse for Jews after a film like this. Besides, Mel Gibson told Fox News that his next project was going to be the story of the Maccabees, so it can't be all bad.

Pulp Fiction (1994, dir. Quentin Tarantino; starring John Travolta and Samuel L. Jackson) Ezekiel is quoted liberally throughout the film, and Jackson's character does not eat pork.

Life of Brian (1979, dir. Terry Jones; starring John Cleese and Michael Palin) At last the truth. Should be seen in a double bill with *The Passion of the Christ*, if possible.

The Big Lebowski (1998, dir. Joel Coen; starring Jeff Bridges and John Goodman) Where else can you find a non-Jewish psychopath who is Shomer Shabbos?

Babe (1995, dir. Chris Noonan; starring a pig) Sales in bacon and ham dropped radically after this movie was screened around the world.

Raid on Entebbe (1977, dir. Irvin Kershner; starring Charles Bronson, Peter Finch—and Martin Balsam) Ah, a time when wearing the IDF uniform and being called Yonni meant you were a hero. Martin Balsam again.

Meet the Parents (2000, dir. Jay Roach; starring Ben Stiller and Robert De Niro) Jew causes chaos in WASP household but still keeps the girl. Unheard of! Unthinkable!

Movies That Are Not Good for the Jews

A Stranger Among Us (1992, dir. Sidney Lumet; starring Melanie Griffith) Words are insufficient to describe this cak.

Jakob the Liar (1999, dir. Peter Kassovitz; starring Robin Williams) It takes some kind of movie to make you want to keep a Jew in the Warsaw Ghetto . . .

Titanic (1997, dir. James Cameron; starring Leonardo DiCaprio and Kate Winslet) No Jews involved here, just a very very bad movie.

Once Upon a Time in America (1984, dir. Sergio Leone; starring Robert De Niro and James Woods) Jewish gangsters? Shame on all those involved. James Woods Jewish? Preposterous.

Protocols of the Elders of Zion Not a movie strictly speaking, more a television miniseries inspired by a best-selling book about the International Jewish Conspiracy which ran on Egyptian National TV a few years ago. TV Series: *A Horseman Without a Horse*, 2002, starring Muhammad Subhi. (Available on Amazon.com, by the way.)

Birth of a Nation (1915, dir. D. W. Griffith; starring Lillian Gish and Ralph Lewis) About the American Civil War and the birth of the Ku Klux Klan. Very popular at Klansmen reunion charity galas.

Se7en (1995, dir. David Fincher; starring Morgan Freeman and Brad Pitt) Not a good movie for Judologists as it casts our sacred number in a poor light.

Keeping the Faith (2000, dir. Edward Norton; starring Ben Stiller and Edward Norton) I lost mine watching this dreck.

Love Story (1970, dir. Arthur Hiller; starring Ryan O'Neal and Ali McGraw) Introduction into the mainstream of the phenomenon that is a Jewish American princess. And he still falls for her . . .

The Chosen (1981, dir. Jeremy Kagan; starring Robby Benson and Rod Steiger) Shhh . . . don't tell everyone.

Nintendo Japanese game company founded in 1889 by Fusajiro Yamauchi. Game Boy, GameCube, Nintendo 64, *Tetris*, *Super Mario Bros*, and their most successful product, Pokémon, are just a few of the 250 games and games systems created by this longest-selling games producer, which has sold over 2 billion games worldwide.

These games must be good for Jewish children as they involve absolutely no physical prowess.

One game in particular, Pokémon, has not been without its share of controversy. Many see it as being part of the Zionist conspiracy. (Then again, many see the weather as being part of the Zionist conspiracy.) Judologists will be disappointed to learn that there is no evidence of the claim that "Goronya" (no.76 in the National Pokédex) is derived from "Golem," the clay monster—created by Rabbi Judah Ben Loew—who terrorized medieval Prague. There is, however, strong suspicion that Perrin Kaplan, currently vice president of Nintendo of America, is Jewish. Certainly sounds Jewish.

Pokémon is a Jewish threat, according to many Muslim leaders, and is banned in many Arab countries. Some have claimed that "Pokémon" means "I am a Jew" in Japanese and believe the toy craze is a demonic Jewish plot to turn Arab children away from Islam. (In fact, "Pokémon" means "pocket monsters" which does not, at first glance, have a strong Jewish etymological link.)

A fatwa, or religious edict, has been issued by a Saudi sheikh arguing that the Pokémon cards bear "six-pointed stars, a symbol of international Zionism and the State of Israel." Sheikh Abdel Moneim Abu Zant, a Saudi religious figure, has declared: "The Pokémon craze is a Jewish plot aimed at forcing our children to forgo their faith and values and to distract them from more important things such as scientific ambitions." If you take away the phrase "a Jewish plot," is there such a huge difference from the kind of argument exercised in many Jewish households?

Surprisingly, only one movie can be found that explores the Jews' relationship with Nintendo. The hit Swedish movie *Bit by Bit* (2002, dir. Jonathan Metzger) explores the terrible choice a young Jew must make between attending the

Nintendo World Cup Games or staying with his family to celebrate Passover. Agony.

backlash		impact		j-factor		tzurus		kabbalah		good/not good
5	+	5	x	4	= 40	÷	7		=	5.7

Nintendo is NOT GOOD FOR THE JEWS

Oral Hygiene and Dentistry Oral hygiene refers to cleanliness of the mouth, particularly the teeth and gums. Keeping the mouth clean by brushing teeth, flossing, and visiting the dentist is the best way to prevent tooth decay, gum disease, and halitosis. The patron saint of dentists is Saint Apollonia, martyred in Alexandria by having all her teeth violently extracted. (source: wikipedia.org)

How many of us have wondered why it costs so much for someone to inflict pain on us, terrorize our children, and play such dreadful Muzak while doing it? It costs around $150 to extract a tooth, an operation that takes the dentist approximately twenty seconds to perform. It seems unfair. Perhaps if they pulled more slowly, patients might feel they're getting their money's worth.

Dentistry has not always been a Jewish preserve; Alpha Omega (founded 1907) is a Jewish dental organization set up in Maryland to fight discrimination in dental schools. Despite the bigotry of earlier years, luminaries in the world of oral hygiene have often been Jews: Theodore Blum, the founder of the New York Institute of Clinical Oral Pathology and Isaac Schour, who used teeth to study systematic disorders. A Jewish dentist was the first to use cocaine—as an anesthetic—in dentistry. Alfred Einhorn, another Jew, then introduced novocaine in 1905. He was sick of the complaints from his neighbors about the snorting noises coming from his lavatories.

Famous Jewish dentists? Leach Cross (a.k.a. Dr. Louis C. Wallach) was a former lightweight champion; Faye Kellerman (*Day of Atonement* and *The Ritual Bath*) is a Jewish mystery author who received a dental degree but never practiced. Goldie Hawn said once all she wanted was to marry "a Jewish dentist." I agree, the list is pretty thin.

What sticks in my craw is when your dentist and his beautiful assistant run out of the room during a radiograph of your teeth. How reassuring it is to hear them sniggering as gamma rays are pumped into your jaw while they shtup in a bath of your dollar bills.

backlash   impact   j-factor   tzurus   kabbalah   good/not good

2.5   +   2.5   x   4   = 20   ÷   7   =   2.86

Oral hygiene and dentistry are NOT GOOD FOR THE JEWS

PDAs Personal Data Assistants, handheld wireless devices that combine cell phone, e-mail, and GPS technology. One of the most popular PDAs is the Blackberry, rumored to have been initially designed for intelligence services and created by Research in Motion (RIM), a Canadian company founded in 1984 by engineering student Mike Lazaridis and Douglas Fregin. The huge popularity of this device has led to accusations of users being "Crackberry addicts" and communicating in jargon like "berry me, honey."

PilotYid is a company that configures Palm Pilots (PDAs) for observant Jews, so now you have no excuse to be late for temple, and if you've missed morning prayers, why not download the Tefilot (prayers) as well as portions of the Talmud and Torah for the superzealous? It also allows downloads of local kosher restaurants (huge demand for this facility) and offers a virtual menorah for those with no time to light the lamp. Paltalk offers an Internet service that provides Torah classes via videoconference, so now you can enjoy your snooze during the rabbi's sermon guilt-free.

Followers of Islam are catered to by companies such as LG Electronics and Dubai-based Ilkone Mobile Telecommunications which make phones that aid Muslims in their daily practice by indicating the direction of Mecca and incorporating the Qur'an within the phone.

This is one case where technology aids religion. Had Moses been given a Blackberry, he could have been spared a second trip up Mount Sinai if Aaron had berried him with "Come back down, the Jews have gone crazy over a cow."

There is nothing inherently Jewish about the PDA aside from the fact that now all mothers can keep track of their sons, no matter what time of day or night. Is it such a crime to stay in touch?

backlash	impact	j-factor	tzurus	kabbalah	good/not good
4.8 +	6.1 x	5.75 =	62.67 ÷	7 =	8.95

PDAs are GOOD FOR THE JEWS

Physical Education Also known as gym class, an integral part of the school curriculum as a means to introduce exercise into children's lives. Inner-city schools are less likely to engage in field sports or cross-country running than rural schools but may engage in more gym-based activities.

The clichéd picture of the bespectacled Jew in stringy vest and patterned shorts hiding wiry legs is clearly erroneous. Some say that exercise to a Jew is like salt to a slug or gefilte fish to a goy—it is simply not meant to be. However, Jews have been successful warriors in the Bible, and in modern times the Israeli Defence Force is feared, so this school of thought is full of holes.

The Jewish reputation for shirking sports and physical education (PE) is more likely to be about the shaming ritual of undressing in the boys' changing rooms. No one needs reminding that the young man was mutilated "down there" as an infant. Also, to some Jews in areas like, say, the Midwest or anywhere in France, disclosure of ethnicity will spell an immediate beating after school.

Perhaps there is also a residual atavistic sense of shame in undressing for exercise? According to the *Encylopedia Judaica*, a gymnasium was built by Jason in Jerusalem in 174 BC, and everyone who used it was obliged to perform in their birthday suits. Some of the Jewish participants, according to I Maccabees 1:15, actually underwent operations for the purpose of concealing the fact that they were circumcised. Reverse circumcision just to get into PE. These biblical Jews were all *meshugge*.

Some great things have happened during PE. Ben and Jerry famously met in junior high gym class in Merrick, Long Island. According to the Ben & Jerry Web site, "Ben Cohen & Jerry Greenfield hated running, but they loved food. In 1978 they decided to go into business together." The rest is history.

A by-product of the Jewish aversion to PE was the mastery of the sick note. This necessitated an overdeveloped medical knowledge in adolescent Jews, which in turn resulted in a high volume of Jewish doctors, thereby contributing immeasurably to general society.

backlash		impact		j-factor		tzurus		kabbalah		good/not good
5.8	+	4.7	x	5.1	= 53.55	÷	7		=	7.65

Physical education is borderline and therefore NOT GOOD FOR THE JEWS

Pope Benedict XVI (born April 16, 1927, as Joseph Alois Ratzinger, in Bavaria, Germany) The 265th reigning pope, the head of the Roman Catholic Church, and the sovereign of Vatican City. He was elected on April 19, 2005, and was enthroned on May 7, 2005.

When Ratzinger turned fourteen he joined the

Hitler Youth. In 1943, Ratzinger was drafted into the Flak (antiaircraft artillery corps). In 1945, days before the German surrender, Ratzinger deserted.

....

A Nazi pope? He joined the Hitler Youth, then the army, and during his time as pope-in-waiting in the early eighties, he becomes the head of the Congregation for the Doctrine of the Faith, the new-and-improved name for the Inquisition. In his book *God and the World* published in 2000, he says, "We wait for the instant in which Israel will say 'yes' to Christ, God and the World." Funny, a lot of people have been waiting for that.

However, in 1936 membership to the Hitler Youth was legally required, and his time in the army did not involve fighting, and he did desert, albeit late in the day. More important, he worked tirelessly behind the scenes to open relations between the Vatican and Israel and he did qualify his position on the thorny issue of Judeo-Christian relations by saying, "The fact Jews don't accept Jesus must not be seen as an act of rejecting God, but as part of God's plan to remind the world that peace and salvation for all humanity has not yet come." (Pontifical Biblical Studies Commission, quoted in *Ha'aretz* newspaper) However, in July 2005 he pointedly omitted naming the Jews as victims of terrorist outrages when he sympathized with "Egypt, Turkey, Iraq, and Great Britain."

His holiness's recent visit to Auschwitz must be viewed

favorably by Judologists. However, it is important to kill the rumor here that as a young cardinal, Ratzinger's absolution advice at Confession included "three Heil Marys."

backlash		impact		j-factor		tzurus		kabbalah		good/not good
5.6	+	6.5	x	4.5	= 54.45 ÷	7	=			7.8

Pope Benedict XVI is borderline and therefore NOT GOOD FOR THE JEWS

Queens The largest of the five boroughs of New York City. In 1898 Queens, Brooklyn, the Bronx, and Staten Island joined up with Manhattan. Queens is the largest borough, mainly residential, and contains a diversity of ethnic minorities. Out of the 2,229,379 residents of this borough today, there are just under 200,000 Jews.

Queens is a good place to die. Many famous Jews are buried in its vast networks of kosher burial grounds. According to the infinitely useful Web site findagrave.com, the following Jews have found peace in the quiet neighborhoods of Queens:

Shalom Aleichem (died 1916) Author whose stories were the basis for Fiddler on the Roof.

Lorenz Hart (died 1943) Lyricist who wrote the lyrics of the musical Pal Joey and songs like "The Lady Is a Tramp."

Harry Houdini (Ehrich Weiss, died 1926) Escapologist. Still waiting for him to reemerge.

Minnie Marx (died 1929) Mother of the Marx Brothers. Of interest to students of comedy.

Alan King (died 2004) Comedian. Of no interest to students of comedy.

Edward G. Robinson (Emmanuel Goldenberg, died 1973) Jew who played at being a mobster.

Louis "Louis Cohen" Kerzner, Jacob "Little Augie" Orgen, Abraham "Kid Twist" Reles, Arnold Rothstein, Abraham Weinberg Jews who did not have to play at being gangsters.

Rabbi Menachem "The Rebbe" Mendel Schneerson, (died 1994) Not a gangster but believed by some to be the Messiah. Like Houdini, we are still waiting for his reappearance.

Barbra Streisand (NDY—not dead yet) Singer and actress. Mount Hebron Cemetery in Flushing is the location of her future burial site. Plot: Section 104, near the road, in case you want visiting practice.

Queens may not be the most exciting borough in New York but it is the most culturally and ethnically diverse. It has a fine history of Jewish residents who have distinguished themselves in the entertainment business: from Simon and Garfunkel to Joey Ramone; from Adrien Brody to Ethel Merman. But it is the fictional home of many more. Archie Bunker, Doug Heffernan, Fran Fine, George Costanza (though there is some dispute over whether one can call this character Jewish). These role models for Jews around the world are all based in Queens. Not only that, there is a sprinkling of glamour to be found in Queens. Peter Parker lived in Queens before he became Spider-Man and even a Hollywood movie was set in this desirable borough—yes, *Coming to America* (starring Eddie Murphy, 1988) was set here, which rather says it all.

Queens is as close to Long Island as you can get. A skip and jump over the Queens-Nassau border, and you are in upward-mobility heaven, Great Neck. All SJQs (Starter Jews from Queens) dream of making the move one day.

However, Great Neck is also a symbol of where Jewish aspiration can go horribly wrong. The Friedman family, exposed in *Capturing the Friedmans*, the award-winning documentary about the most dsyfunctional Jewish family on Earth, lived in Great Neck. After this film was released, rumors of a name change for the town to Leap Frog were quickly dismissed.

Brooklyn, which might have made a more obvious choice, was not chosen for this section because:

1. *The Crown Heights riots of 1991 were Not Good for the Jews*

2. *Brooklyn does not begin with the letter "Q"*

backlash		*impact*		*j-factor*		*tzurus*		*kabbalah*		*good/not good*
3.5	+	4.5	x	6.75	=	54	÷	7	=	7.71

Queens is borderline and therefore NOT GOOD FOR THE JEWS

⋯⋯⋯⋯⋯⋯⋯⋯⋯⋯⋯⋯⋯⋯⋯⋯⋯⋯⋯⋯⋯⋯⋯⋯⋯

QVC "QVC is a virtual shopping mall where customers can shop for quality merchandise 24 hours a day, 7 days a week, 364 days a year via television, telephone, or computer," according to its Web site. It claims to obtain products from "every continent on the globe except Antarctica." QVC ("Quality, Value, and Convenience") was founded in 1986 by Joseph M. Segel, founder of the Franklin Mint. Its customer base is now 141 million.

⋯⋯⋯⋯⋯⋯⋯⋯⋯⋯⋯⋯⋯⋯⋯⋯⋯⋯⋯⋯⋯⋯⋯⋯⋯

Surely the Jews have outgrown their reputation for being voracious shoppers? The old jokes once heard on the lawns of Jewish golf clubs—"My wife and I always hold hands. If I let go, she shops"; "My wife has a black belt in shopping"; "My wife wants to be buried at the mall. That way, she knows the children will visit"—must be a thing of the past?

Sadly, evidence shows that there is still a strong affinity between Jews and the art of shopping. HSN, the Home Shopping Network, pioneer in the field and inspiration for QVC, did originate in Florida. There have been moves to help young Jews assuage their insatiable appetites for retail. For example, in the famous English castle town of York, the council planned to build a huge shopping center on the mass grave site of Jews massacred in 1190. What next? A Disney store in Dachau? One way of stopping Jews from shopping.

Another technique to thwart the OJS (Obsessive Jewish Shopper) was adopted by Iran in the nineteenth century. According to the travel writer J. J. Benjamin, Jews were forbidden to inspect any goods in a shop; if an item was touched, the Jewish customer was required to purchase it at any quoted price. This kind of torture is barbaric. Thank goodness the situation for Jews in Iran has vastly improved since those dark times.

Is QVC Jewish? Well, Barry Diller steered the good ship during the nineties, and Comcast, its majority shareholder today, is run by Brian Roberts (son of Ralph J.), a great Jewish philanthropist and entrepreneur. Uri Geller and Joan Rivers have sold their jewelry lines on the channel to great success, but please do not be misled: non-Jews *are* allowed to buy and sell on QVC. However, things did go slightly awry in 1994 when the U.S. Department of Justice filed a lawsuit against the company for shady claims over a weight-loss product. Weight-loss products on a Jewish channel! How *narish* can you be? I ask you. It's like selling a swimsuit to an Eskimo.

backlash	impact	j-factor	tzurus	kabbalah	good/not good
4.6	+ 4.5	x 6.1	= 55.51	÷ 7	= 7.93

QVC is borderline and therefore NOT GOOD FOR THE JEWS

Rhinoplasty A surgical procedure, usually performed to enhance the appearance of the nose. Jacques Joseph (1865–1934), born Jakob Lewin Joseph in Königsberg, Prussia, second son of Rabbi Israel Joseph, was one of the fathers of modern plastic surgery who developed methods for aesthetic plastic surgery. He believed that the way someone looks can affect their happiness and social prospects. Such disadvantages could be relieved by the cosmetic changes afforded by rhinoplasty. (source: wikipedia.org)

"Everybody wanted to look like a shiksa," said Dr. Thomas D. Rees, a retired plastic surgeon (Jane Gross, *New York Times*), about those heady boom years of rhinoplasty in the seventies. Though the numbers have declined since then, this controversial choice of bat mitzvah gift is still a sore point in the Jewish community.

Could it be said that the nose job is a defining anti-Semitic act? The fact that it was pioneered by Jews whose clientele were primarily other Jews does not alleviate the seriousness of the charge of Uncle Tomism—or Uncle Hymieism, as it is known in some parts.

But is there such a thing as a Jewish Nose? And if not, is the nose job Good or Bad for the Jews? Anti-Semitic literature is full of detailed diagrams of "the Jewish Nose" (see below), and therefore to acknowledge its existence is Not Good for the Jews, but can its removal in surgery be seen as Bad for the Jews?

> CLASS IV. THE JEWISH, or Hawk Nose, is very convex, and preserves its convexity like a bow, throughout the whole length from the eyes to the tip. It is thin and sharp.
>
> It indicates considerable Shrewdness in worldly matters; a deep Insight into character, and facility of turning that insight to profitable account.

(source: *Notes on Noses* by George Jabet, published London, 1852)

The "Jewish Nose" has proved an asset to some people. Barbra Streisand was famously conflicted over whether to tame her schnozzle but ultimately realized it was her trademark. Jennifer Grey, star of *Dirty Dancing* with Patrick Swayze, had no such qualms and subsequently fatally damaged her career by shaving her cartilages. By her own admission, she "began to look like that girl out of *Dirty Dancing*, but not quite" (Channel 5 interview in United Kingdom, 2005). A sober warning to Jews everywhere: Don't cut off your nose to spite your career.

backlash		impact		j-factor		tzurus		kabbalah		good/not good
7	+	5	x	6	=	72	÷	7	=	11.1

Rhinoplasty is GOOD FOR THE JEWS

....

Rock 'n' Roll Arguably, the most influential of all musical genres, rock 'n' roll had its heyday in fifties America and emerged as a term from the phenomenon of black artists who seemingly "rocked" while singing gospel. It found its zenith with Elvis Presley's first recording, "That's All Right (Mama)," in 1954. Although it takes many forms—rhythm and blues, heavy metal, surf, gospel, Christian, punk, Britpop, grunge, garage, folk, and so on—it is best identified by its reliance on guitar and heavy beat.

....

For an accurate analysis of whether Rock 'n' Roll is Good for the Jews, one need look no further than at the King of Rock,

Elvis Presley. In the recent documentary *Schmelvis: Searching for the King's Jewish Roots*, evidence is shown that Elvis was Jewish. His maternal great-great-grandmother, Nancy Tackett, née Burdine, was believed to have been Jewish. Elvis had many Jewish friends as a boy growing up in Memphis. So close to the Jewish community was he, in fact, that he was said to have had the honor of being the "Shabbos Goy" for Rabbi Alfred Fruchter, who lived upstairs from him. Mrs. Fruchter has said that he was a "particularly big fan of matzoh ball soup and challah." Later in life, he wore a Star of David side by side with his cross around his neck. This could have been a severe case of hedging one's bets, but let us assume it was due to his natural affinity for Jews.

However, one slip on the Judological scale must be the recording of "Edelweiss" while serving in the U.S. Army in Germany. Not necessary.

Many of Elvis's hits were written by Jerry Leiber and Mike Stoller ("Hound Dog," "Jailhouse Rock," and many more) and many Jews were involved in his biggest hits ("King Creole," "Treat Me Nice," "Stuck on You," "Good Luck Charm," "Big Hunk o 'Love," "It's Now or Never," "Surrender," "Viva Las Vegas," "Suspicion," and others).

The history of rock is peppered with Jewish influence, as the following list shows:

Jews Who Rock, or the Shul of Rock

Michael Bolton (born Michael Bolotin) OK, not a great start, but the man with the hair has sold a lot of records.

Mick Jones of the Clash Known for their progressive views on race relations, the Clash were an important influence on punk rock. Still, did they need to be so rude?

Sammy Davis Jr. Cool Jew.

Neil Diamond He wrote the song "I'm a Believer" for the Monkees. Such a nice Jewish boy. Also wrote "My Name Is Yussel" for his movie version of The Jazz Singer, which was frankly pushing it.

Phil Spector Despite describing his music as "Wagnerian," Phil followed the Irving Berlin school of making money by producing hit Xmas albums like A Christmas Gift to You and Santa Claus Is Coming to Town.

Lenny Kravitz A great friend of Michael Jackson, his seventh album was titled Baptism, which does not augur well.

Beck A Scientologist now, but we can still call him a Jew.

Lou Reed (father's name: Rabinowitz) Brought transsexuals into the mainstream. Famously no great fan of Dylan and was heard to have said about him, "If you were at a party with him, you'd have to tell him to shut up." Sacrilege!

Billy Joel Almost raised as a Catholic, and many confuse his ethnicity with Italian, but there should be no confusion when his choice of second wife is analyzed. This troubled talent from the Bronx wed an Uptown Girl, all-American Christie Brinkley, who looked so blond and non-Jewish that many realized Billy must be a Jew to want her so much.

Gene Simmons Born Chaim Witz in Israel, he found love with a blond all-American *Playboy* model. Is there a theme here?

Barry Manilow There is some doubt about whether Mr. Manilow is, in fact, Jewish. Just kidding.

Kenny G (born Kenneth Gorelich) Holds the world record for blowing an E on his sax for forty-five minutes. And people pay for this? Feh!

Kinky Friedman His hit, "They Ain't Makin' Jews Like Jesus Anymore," sung with his backing group, the Texas Jewboys, is a high point in Jewish rock. Kinky ran for Texas governor under the slogan "Kinky Friedman: Why the Hell Not?"

Beastie Boys Licensed to Ill *is a great name for a rap album by Jews and deserved its place as rap's first U.S. number-one album in 1987.*

Matisyahu Not yet a household name, but this reggae rocker, a Lubavitcher Hasid from Crown Heights, has already been profiled in Rolling Stone *magazine, has appeared on MTV, and has been named by the* Forward *as one of the five most influential Jews in America. (source: jewsrock.org)*

The phenomenon of JuMu (Jewish music and secular rock) has grown in recent years, with Hip Hop Hoodios and DJ Peretz exemplifying the trend.

backlash		impact		j-factor		tzurus		kabbalah		good/not good
4.1	+	6.6	x	5.6	=	59.9	÷	7	=	8.6

Rock 'n' Roll is GOOD FOR THE JEWS

World Timeline
(Part IV–1750 to 2006)

World				
1789	1794	1803	1848	1865
French Revolution begins George Washington becomes president	Whiskey Rebellion erupts over liquor taxes	United States purchases Louisiana from French for $15 million, doubling the size of U.S. territory	Karl Marx writes *Communist Manifesto*	American Civil War ends Lincoln shot at Ford's Theatre

Jewish				
1789	1794	1803	1848	1865
Prices slashed in half for weekend trips to Paris First landslide victory. Got so many votes, they named the town after him	Jews don't drink, so no issue here	Now that is a sweet kosher deal	*Duck Soup* is smash hit on Broadway	Pretty Uncivil, if you ask me First run of *The Producers* ends

1897	1912	1923	1948
First Zionist Congress	*Titanic* sinks	*Mein Kampf* written by Adolf Hitler	Ghandi murdered, leading to chaos in India

1897	1912	1923	1948
Jewish mating ritual	Jews blamed—Greenberg, Goldberg, iceberg, same difference	The musical version, *Oy, Have I Got Problems!* fails to get backers	Terrible shame, but Israel is created!

World

1969	1970s	1980s	1990s	2000-2006
Man lands on Moon	Nixon's rise and fall Arabs and Israelis kill each other for another decade Scorsese, Coppola, and Altman dominate American cinema	Reagan era Cold War ends	Bush Sr. in power Clinton era	Bush Jr. in power Second war on Iraq Osama bin Laden still at large

Jewish

1969	1970s	1980s	1990s	2000-2006
NJI (no Jews involved)	Carl Bernstein gets a break Begin and Sadat win Nobel Peace Prize Woody Allen's *Annie Hall* beats *Star Wars* for best picture Oscar (1977)	Reagan very popular with Jews until he paid his respects at Bitburg cemetery—an SS graveyard Berlin Wall crashes down and lets rabid anti-Semites back into the West	Bush loses Jewish vote when he says he was one guy against thousands of Jewish lobbies—big no no Cigar sales rise 1000 percent	God told Bush to invade Iraq. God tells Jews to vote Democrat next time At least when the Israelis bombed the Osirak nuclear reactors in 1981, they were there Jews blamed

Schwarzenegger, Arnold (born 1947, in Thal, Austria) After serving a mandatory year in the Austrian army, Schwarzenegger became a bodybuilder and subsequently left Austria for Hollywood to make his name in the movies. He was not successful until he made *Conan the Barbarian* in 1982 and then went on to star in numerous action films, such as *The Last Action Hero* (1993) and the Terminator films (1984, 1991, 2003), and comedies such as *Twins* (1988), *Kindergarden Cop* (1990), and *Junior* (1994). He was elected governor of California in 2003.

There is some discussion about how big a Nazi Arnie's father, Gustav Schwarzenegger, really was. The Wiesenthal Center claims there was no evidence that he was a war criminal—and that has nothing to do with the $750,000 Arnie donated to the center—but according to the *Los Angeles Times* (August 14, 2003), Schwarzenegger Sr. was indeed a member of the SA, also known as the Brown Shirts. He joined Hitler's henchmen quite late in the day, on May 1, 1939—about six months after Kristallnacht, so it is unlikely he joined just because of the nice uniform.

Arnie was also good friends with Kurt Waldheim, the controversial ex-Nazi, former UN secretary general, and Austrian president. You can't help it if your mates just happen to be ex-Nazis (or your dad, come to that), but then I don't suppose you need to invite high-profile war criminals to your wedding (summer 1986) and then spend most of your wedding speech extolling his great Austrian qualities (or "Kvalities").

Good ol' Arnie isn't shy of courting anti-Semites. In 1996 he was seen enjoying the company of Jörg Haider, the leader of the Austrian extreme right-wing Freedom Party, and there is, of course, his famous comment to reporters after the release of the movie *Pumping Iron* in 1976, in which he expressed admiration for good ol' Adolf; news stories quoted him as saying that he "admired Hitler's rise to power and wished he could have experienced the thrill the Nazi leader must have had holding sway over huge audiences." Since he has become Republican governor of California, he has strangely dropped his Hitler impressions and courting of extremists. In fact, he helped launch plans for a Museum of Tolerance in Jerusalem and is very popular with Jews in California.

Judologists should note that Governor Schwarzenegger has a pig-heart valve, which might be another cause for concern.

backlash		impact		j-factor		tzurus		kabbalah		good/not good
4.6	+	3.7	x	3.6	= 29.9	÷	7	=		4.3

Arnold Schwarzenegger is NOT GOOD FOR THE JEWS

Scientology, the Church of Scientology was first developed in the United States in the 1950s by the author of *Dianetics*, L. Ron Hubbard (1922–1986). Hubbard was virulently opposed to all forms of psychotherapy and designed Scientology as an alternative that would help humans develop their spirit through counseling (known as "auditing") and rehabilitation. Scientology maintains that humans are spiritual beings (known as "thetans") who lived through many past lives and will continue to live after the death of our bodies. The church promises to help teach people how to achieve the ultimate goal of getting the thetan back to its original state of freedom. The more advanced teachings are kept strictly confidential from new initiates and reserved for those who are "spiritually prepared." To this day, there continues to be some controversy over whether it is a religion or not.

Scientology does have a litigious reputation, and Jon Stewart's popular *Daily Show* is rumored to have a "no Scientology jokes" policy because of this. A religion that can't laugh at itself is, well, frankly, not Jewish.

Scientology has had harsh critics in its short life—none more so than the German government. Claudia Nolte, the minister of family policy, described the church as "one of the most aggressive groups in our society," and charges of corruption and gross commercialism have been made by the German establishment.

L. Ron Hubbard had some, shall we say, "old-fashioned" views on race relations, and his negative stance on psychotherapy remains controversial. In 2005 Tom Cruise had a very public spat with Brooke Shields over her postnatal blues. This "debate" about whether Ms. Shields should or should not have used antidepressants did not garner positive PR on behalf of the multimillion-dollar religion. However, any movement that provides a cheaper alternative to shrink fees can't be all bad.

backlash		impact		j-factor		tzurus		kabbalah		good/not good
3.05	+	4.15	x	1	=	7.2	÷	7	=	1.03

The Church of Scientology is NOT GOOD FOR THE JEWS

Six Degrees of Separation A parlor game where you can connect any famous person by six stages to you or someone equally obscure or incongruous. For example, finding six links from the pope to the chief rabbi of Israel. Two versions of this game are provided here for Judologists. Both are circular (starting with someone famous and coming full circle back to that person by the end), but feel free to insert your own destination point. The game was developed into Six Degrees of Kevin Bacon after it was discovered that he has appeared in so many movies that he can be connected to every actor on Earth.

Six Degrees of Larry David*
(using Jews only)

1. *Larry David appeared in a cameo role in* Radio Days, *a movie by Woody Allen.*

2. *Woody Allen learned his craft in the fifties with top comic Sid Caesar.*

3. *Sid Caesar discovered Mel Brooks on his* Show of Shows.

* Apologies to Kevin Bacon, who, for obvious reasons, could not be part of this game.

4. Mel Brooks cast Zero Mostel in his movie version of The Producers.

5. Zero Mostel's character, Max Bialystock, was played in the theatrical production by Jason Alexander.

6. Jason Alexander played George Costanza in Seinfeld, a character based on Larry David.

Judologists prefer Seven Degrees, as the number 7 is more spiritual. The rules of this version are less stringent, and non-Jews can be used. For example:

Seven Degrees of Woody Allen

1. Woody Allen's muse in his recent movies is Scarlett Johansson.

2. Scarlett Johansson's early movie Eight Legged Freaks starred David Arquette.

3. David Arquette is married to Courteney Cox, star of Scream and Friends.

4. Courteney Cox sprang to fame after being pulled from a crowd by Bruce Springsteen in his video for "Dancing in the Dark."

5. *Bruce Springsteen wrote the song "Shut Out the Light" for the movie* Born on the Fourth of July, *starring Tom Cruise.*

6. *Tom Cruise had a row about Scientology with Scarlett Johansson, forcing her to pull out of* Mission Impossible III.

7. *Scarlett Johansson is the new muse of Woody Allen.*

Please feel free to play this at home using other famous Jewish and Gentile names. I would like to suggest the following for beginners:

> **Dov Ber Borochov** *Pioneer of early Zionism—six degrees to Dean Martin.*
>
> **The Baal Shem Tov** *Founder of Hasidism—six degrees to Britney Spears.*
>
> **God** *Prime Mover and Creator of Everything—six degrees to Donald Trump. Only joking, that would be impossible. Try W. C. Fields.*

Oodles of fun for the Judologist on a break from his or her calculations.

....

Star Trek Gene Roddenberry created this huge television, publishing, and movie franchise. The original *Star*

Trek TV series aired between 1966 and 1969 on the NBC network. Although spin-off series were developed in the nineties, the original science fiction TV series with its eighty episodes remains most popular. The show depicts the journeys of the USS *Enterprise*, whose mission is "to boldly go where no man has gone before" and seek out new civilizations while promoting peace and understanding throughout the galaxy.

Though created by a non-Jew, *Star Trek* eerily contains many Jewish components and themes. Aside from the obvious—USS *Enterprise* is hardly the name of a non-Jewish spaceship, is it?—several key cast members are Jewish: William Shatner (Captain Kirk), Leonard Nimoy (Spock), and Walter Koenig (Chekov). Spock's Vulcan greeting was invented by Leonard Nimoy based on his memories of shul, where he was asked to perform the ritual blessing of the Kohanim (the priests) and learned the secret sign. (Some Trekkies believe that *The Wrath of Khan*, the movie, had its title changed by Nimoy from "The Wrath of Kohen.") Other obvious parallels between Vulcans and Jews: big ears instead of big noses; great powers of assimilation as outsiders (aliens, in fact); both are very brainy; and both peoples are good at chess.

Spock was, of course, only half Vulcan—his father was Vulcan and his mother was human. Unlike Orthodox Jews, Vulcan culture is not strictly matrilineal, and Spock considered himself Vulcan even though his mother wasn't one. There is no evidence as to whether Spock had trouble getting his children into the best Vulcan schools (there is a long waiting list for VFS—Vulcan Free School) as a result of this, but there is considerable proof to support the argument that Spock's parents were not frummie Vulcans.

The one strange anomaly in this argument was that the doctor, Bones, was not Jewish. Whoever heard of a non-Jewish doctor?

Backlash		impact		j-factor		tzurus		kabbalah		good/not good
4	+	6	x	6	= 60	÷	7	=		8.57

Star Trek is GOOD FOR THE JEWS

....

Star Wars The generic name for George Lucas's sextet of movies (the original, two sequels, and three prequels). The original was released in 1977, and the cycle ended in 2005 with *Revenge of the Sith*. A classic good-versus-evil story line reworked as a futuristic, intergalactic epic. *Star Wars* tells of the struggle between the Rebel Alliance and the Galactic Empire thousands of years in the future. The protagonist of the first movie is the young Luke Skywalker, who leaves his home planet, teams up with other rebels, and tries to save Princess Leia, who is being held captive by the evil Darth Vader. *Star Wars* was, at the time of its release, the biggest grossing movie of all time

Lucas is neither Jewish nor German, but the Jewish references are many. For Galactic Empire read the Weimar Republic; a chancellor issuing emergency decrees and pronouncing himself emperor forever rings a faint bell with those who remember a certain historical figure in the first half of the twentieth century; even more subtle is the name of the emperor's personal guards—stormtroopers; both emperors lose wars, and eventually the dicatorships they turn their empires into become republics again; and to round it off, we have segregated parts of Coruscant for all non-human species—nothing at all like ghettos for Untermenschen.

However, certain *Star Wars* commentators have expressed concern over the character Watto the Toydarian. A slave trader with hideous hooked nose, strong shtetlized Eastern European accent, and abominable teeth, bent on destroying the beautiful blond Annakin—might he be seen as an anti-Semitic stereotype?

Other experts argue the contrary and provide proof that *Star Wars* is in fact a Jewish text. Obi-wan Kenobi is also known as Ben Kenobi. A *navi* is a prophet in Hebrew—ahem, isn't that his role?

But the slam dunk on this issue must be the first scene in *Star Wars* when C3PO and R2D2 are wandering (get the reference?) on Tatooine. C3PO bemoans his fate: "We seem to be made to suffer. That's our lot in life." Surely, Jewish robots.

backlash	impact	j-factor	tzurus	kabbalah	good/not good
5.5 +	5.1 x	6.1 =	64.66 ÷	7 =	9.24

Star Wars *is GOOD FOR THE JEWS*

Stiller, Ben (born November 30, 1965, in New York) Hollywood actor/director, best known for comedy roles in *Zoolander* (2001), which he wrote and directed, *Reality Bites* (1994), which he also directed, *There's Something About Mary* (1998), *Meet the Parents* (2000), and *Meet the Fockers* (2004).

Hollywood's rent-a-Jew? Gaylord "Greg" Focker in *Meet the Parents* and *Meet the Fockers*, Reuben Feffer in *Along Came Polly*, and Rabbi Jake Schram in *Keeping the Faith*—even when not specifically Jewish, he is always Jewish. See, for example, *Reality Bites*, *The Royal Tenenbaums*, and *There's Something About Mary*. He has managed to convey the Jew on-screen as fractionally less nerdy (he works out) and not as irritating as Ross in *Friends* or Woody Allen in any of his last seven movies.

His father is Jerry Stiller, who is a regular on the sitcom *The King of Queens*, often appeared on *Seinfeld*, and had a popular comedy duo with his wife, Anne Meara (Miranda's mother-in-law on *Sex and the City*). He played the funny Jewish guy and she his Irish bride. Which was true. She was born Catholic but converted to Judaism six years after marrying Jerry.

Despite Stiller's success and his overt Jewishness, people still like him. Even in the Midwest, where they don't like Jews, they do like Ben Stiller—*Zoolander* did extremely well at the box office there. But Stiller does have his critics. David Denby wrote in the *New Yorker*, "Stiller is the latest, and crudest, version of the urban Jewish male on the make." He's been labeled the Paul Michael Glaser of the twenty-first century, but a Jew playing the lead who doesn't have to look like Paul Newman or Kirk Douglas is a step in the right direction, no?

Perhaps Stiller's marriage to a model who is both blond and called Christine causes Jews to feel conflicted—between jealousy and envy. In fact, several of Stiller's characters go for blonds like Teri Polo in *Meet the Parents*, Jenna Elfman in *Keeping the Faith*, and a blondish Jennifer Aniston in *Along Came Polly*, where Jewish alternative girlfriends are dumped in favor of all-American non-Jewesses. He does fall for a Jewish leading lady in *Reality Bites*—Winona Ryder (Horowitz)—but the movie received only cult status. The pursuit of the shiksa is one of the great Hollywood themes and has nothing to do with unhappily married Jewish movie executives acting out their fantasies.

backlash		impact		j-factor		tzurus		kabbalah		good/not good
5	+	5	x	7	=	70	÷	7	=	10

Ben Stiller is GOOD FOR THE JEWS

Sudoku A number puzzle consisting of a nine-by-nine-square grid that is subdivided into three-by-three subgrids. Each row, column, and subgrid must contain the numbers 1 through 9. Sudoku puzzles appear with a few numbers already filled in—the puzzle solver must use these to work out where all the other numbers go.

This type of puzzle was first created by Leonhard Euler, a Swiss mathematician, in 1776. In 1984, the leading puzzle company in Japan, Nikoli, discovered the puzzles and began publishing them under the name Suuji Wa Dokushin Ni Kagiru which means "the numbers must occur only once." They became very popular, one of the best-selling puzzles in Japan, and in 1986 the president of Nikoli shortened the name to Sudoku (*su* means number and *doku* means single).

The Sudoku virus hit the West in November 2004, when the *Times* of London printed its first puzzle. It spread to New York in April 2005, when the *New York Post* adopted it, followed by *USA Today*, spurring over one hundred international best-selling books.

Is Sudoku Good for the Jews? Aside from sounding like tzedakah (charity), any puzzle that uses numbers is good for the Judologist (although a slight disappointment must be expressed that 9 is the chosen number, and not 7). Some shame and slight embarrassment must be expressed that no Jewish links can be made to the creation of this numerical craze. However, Jews should be good at number games. They have enough experience with charging by the hour. It is no accident that the fourth book of Moses is called Numbers.*

As we know, Gematriya (numerical value of Hebrew letters) is a central plank of Talmudic learning and therefore should prove good training to Sudokists. According to Jeremy Maissel of the *Jerusalem Post*, we can put "Sudoku itself to the gematriya test. Sudoku totals 182, the equivalent of *holech vehazek*—getting stronger and stronger—which characterizes the popularity of the new craze and reassuringly confirms the authentic significance of gematriya." Wise words.

Downside? To make room for Sudoku, newspapers are shedding their bridge columns, which is catastrophic for the Jews of Florida.

*Plans to bring out the Institute's version, Judoku, have been temporarily stalled due to a severe lack of demand, but a book of puzzles should be ready in time for the Christmas 2007 market.

backlash		impact		j-factor		tzurus		kabbalah		good/not good
3.4	+	6.6	x	5.25	= 70.35	÷	7		=	10.05

Sudoku is GOOD FOR THE JEWS

Tattoos The word *tattoo* is derived from the Tahitian *tatu,* which means "to mark something." The earliest identified tattoos are from Ancient Egypt, though it has been claimed that tattooing has existed since 12,000 BC. Tattoos are more popular now than at any time in recorded history. According to current estimates, one in seven, or over 39 million people, in North America has at least one tattoo.

The Old Testament tells us that tattoos are Bad for the Jews. Hidden away in the book of Leviticus, snuggled neatly after the legal quagmire of crossbreeding animals, lies the decree: "Ye shall not make any cuttings in your flesh for the dead, nor print any marks upon you" (Leviticus 19:28). Maimonides, the great scholar, took a dim view of tattooing, saying it was a pretty pagan thing to do: "This was the custom of the gentiles that they inscribe themselves for idol worship." Even though the myth that Jews with tattoos will not be buried in a Jewish cemetery has been dispelled, why do so many Jews love to defile themselves so?

Perhaps the greatest living Jewish advocate of the ancient art is David Beckham, Britain's most famous soccer player and captain of the English team, who has nine tattoos. In November 2000, he had tattooed the name of his wife—Spice Girl Victoria Beckham—spelled in Hindi. Beckham was soon to learn that the artist had in fact spelled out "Vihctoria." Not quite as bad as JFK's gaffe, "Ich bin ein Berliner" (translation: "I am a jam doughnut"), but a pretty strong contender. Seemingly unconcerned about his lack of talent with languages, he followed this with a Latin phrase on his left forearm and, most recently, a phrase in Hebrew from the Shir Hashirim ("Song of Songs"). "I am for my beloved and my beloved is for me" is what he thinks it says. "Don't fancy yours much, mate" is a closer translation.

Women with tattoos have traditionally been highly attractive to Jewish men. After all, they must be experienced in making decisions they regret later.

Celebrities and tattoos have a long history. Jewish celebrities discovering their Jewishness and expressing it in this ironically sinful way are another phenomenon. When

Courtney Love discovered that she was not in fact Irish but Jewish, she was rumored to have undertaken the painful process of having the shamrock tattoos removed from her breasts.

backlash		impact		j-factor		tzurus		kabbalah		good/not good
2	+	2	x	2	=	8	÷	7	=	1.14

Tattoos are NOT GOOD FOR THE JEWS

....

TiVo A popular brand of digital video recorder that allows the user to store television programs to an internal hard drive for later viewing. One of its most popular features is its selection of the programming based on the user's past preferences. Additionally, programs being watched "live" can be paused or "rewound" to repeat a sequence just watched. The device was created by TiVo Inc., a company started by veterans of Silicon Graphics and Time Warner's Full Service Network digital video system.

....

This simple device has revolutionized the lives of millions of Jews around the world. Only now can you pause a live game on TV to finish that raging argument with your spouse or children and not ruin the enjoyment of live sport. Also, crucially, the male of the house is able to fast-forward all commercial breaks, saving himself thousands of dollars in domestic products that his wife now cannot see. In religious or observant Jewish families, the TiVo is known affectionately as the "Shabbos Goy" (traditionally, local non-Jews were employed to use electrical goods as Jews were prohibited from doing so under the laws of the Sabbath).

A man called his rabbi and said, "I know tonight is Kol Nidre, the holiest night in the Jewish calendar, but the Yankees start the playoffs. Rabbi, I've got to watch the Yankee game on TV." "Aha," the Rabbi responded. "That's what TiVo is for." The man was impressed. "You mean I can record Kol Nidre?"

Possibly, the most compelling argument why TiVo is Good for the Jews must lie in its magical "Season Pass Manager" facility. This allows the viewer to pick an automatic function that records all the series of any particular show by one hit of the button. By simply looking in the documentaries section and selecting "documentaries," you can have all possible programs on World War II recorded for you at any time of day or night. Unfortunately, there is no ability yet to program "Jew-only" commands.

TiVo is the ultimate tool for the serious Judologist.

backlash		impact		j-factor		tzurus		kabbalah		good/not good
3.45	+	5.2	x	6.66	= 57.61	÷	7	=		8.23

TiVo is GOOD FOR THE JEWS

Trial of Michael Jackson, the (born Michael Joseph Jackson on August 29, 1958, in Gary, Indiana) The so-called "King of Pop" was performing by the age of six as the lead singer and youngest member of the Jackson 5. He began his solo career in 1979 with the album *Off the Wall* and achieved global fame with the 1982 album *Thriller*. The June 2005 trial began after ABC's broadcast of the documentary *Living with Michael Jackson*, in which Brit journalist Martin Bashir got Jackson to admit to sharing his bed with boys. One of those boys, a recovering cancer patient, claimed that Mr. Jackson had showed him pornography and plied him with alcohol. Mr. Jackson was arrested and indicted on ten counts, including lewd acts on a child and supplying alcohol to a minor. He was cleared of all charges.

Michael Jackson is not shy when it comes to expressing his feelings about Jews. *Good Morning America* aired (November 2005) a two-year-old answering machine message on which Mr. Jackson alledgedly ranted on about Jews as "leeches" and being part of a "conspiracy." Mind you, this is from the great lyricist whose 1995 hit "They Don't Care About Us" included the wonderful rhyme "Jew me, sue me" before it was removed following protests from the Anti-Defamation League.

Surprising, then, to discover that so many Jews have been employed by him and have leapt to his side during times of trouble. Benjamin Brafman was part of his defense team (he is best-known for winning an acquittal in 2001 for Sean "P Diddy" Combs on bribery and weapons charges). The actor Corey Feldman, the Rabbi Shmuley Boteach, and the paranormalist Uri Geller—all embarrassed themselves by supporting Jackson before the trial.

Concern must be raised over his choice of the hotel where his entourage stayed during the trial. The Chumash Casino, where MJ also held his victory celebration after being cleared of the charges, does sound pretty Jewish, but Chumash is actually the name of the local Indian tribe that runs the casino rather than the five books of the Torah, but no smoke without fire, et cetera. There were rumors that the notoriously anti-Semitic Nation of Islam would be playing a significant role in MJ's affairs, but this has been denied by Nation spokespeople. In fact, they were insulted by the slur.

backlash		*impact*		*j-factor*		*tzurus*		*kabbalah*		*good/not good*
3	+	5	x	4.5	=	36	÷	7	=	5.1

The trial of Michael Jackson is NOT GOOD FOR THE JEWS

USA PATRIOT Act, the Passed by Congress in the aftermath of 9/11 in October 2001, the act grants the federal government increased power to access private records, conduct secret searches, and detain and deport noncitizens. Highly controversial, this act was rushed through Congress with little time for public debate or discussion.

USA PATRIOT stands for "Uniting and Strengthening America by Providing Appropriate Tools Required to Intercept and Obstruct Terrorism." Also known as "Unless Somebody Asks, People Are Treasonous Rogues Intent on Terror."

Jews tend to be split on this issue. On the one hand, Jews

have always been at the forefront of the war against infringements of civil liberties, but this law could be said to protect Jews from attacks in places where Jews congregate in large numbers, such as temples, community centers, and shopping malls. Besides, when was snooping on your neighbor a criminal offense? Without gossip and rumor, even fewer Jews would attend synogogue during the High Holy Days.

As nobody has really read the whole act, nobody really knows how much of it is simply uncontroversial updates to preexisting privacy laws in response to technological change and how much of it empowers an opportunistic administration bent on crushing all civil liberties to usher in a new McCarthy era.

By far the most compelling argument for the PATRIOT Act comes from Rabbi David Feldman, a spokesperson for Jews Against Anti-Semitism. He states, "Under Section 802 of the 2001 USA PATRIOT Act, any crime which endangers human life is defined as an act of domestic terrorism. Mel Gibson's incitement of anti-Semitism is a civil disobedience crime which endangers human life, and under the PATRIOT Act, his creation of the movie *The Passion of the Christ* is an act of domestic terrorism." Who could argue with that?

backlash		impact		j-factor		tzurus		kabbalah		good/not good
7	+	5	x	1	=	12	÷	7	=	1.71

The USA PATRIOT Act is NOT GOOD FOR THE JEWS

Viagra The FDA describes Viagra as such:

> Viagra is a prescription medicine taken by mouth for
> the treatment of erectile dysfunction (ED) in men.
> ED is a condition where the penis does not harden
> and expand when a man is sexually excited, or when
> he cannot keep an erection. Viagra may help a man
> with ED get and keep an erection when he is sexually
> excited.

The Jewish attitude toward the sex act has long been the
butt of jokes. A religious couple, about to marry, ask their
rabbi if they are allowed to dance together at weddings?

"Categorically, *no*," says the rabbi. "What about sex? Are the rules as harsh once we are married?" "You *must* have sex! It's a mitzvah," the rabbi replies. "Different positions?" they timidly ask. "Absolutely, in fact the Torah commands the Jewish man to pleasure the Jewish woman at all times." "Even doggie position?" "Whatever you want." "Woman on top?" "Why not," the rabbi responds without flinching. "Standing up?" the couple ask. "Absolutely not!" the rabbi shouts. "Why ever not?" the young man asks. "It might lead to dancing," the rabbi replies.

Now that Jewish couples have had the good news that Viagra is kosher for Passover (a ruling in 1998 allowed its use after some discussion over whether the coating of the pills was nonkosher), in Israel a prescription for Viagra, according to BBC News, is issued once every minute. Rabbis encourage congregants to use the wonder drug because procreation is Good for the Jews. No surprise, then, to discover that one of the key scientists behind its invention at Pfizer was a Jew called Robert Furchgott.

As we've said, Jews and sex are strange bedfellows. There are many jokes about how rare the act is in Jewish homes, and yet the evidence is otherwise. Jews have always played a large part in the adult film industry in America. Reuben Sturman, the "Disney of Double Penetration," was a notorious purveyor of filth, controlling a large part of the industry in seventies. Steven Hirsch runs Vivid Entertainment Group, the Paramount of Porn, and Seymore Butts (Adam

Glasser) owns and operates the top Indie brand, the Miramax of Masturbation. These are just three Jewish pioneers in this much maligned business—without Viagra to encourage performers, where would this vital Jewish business be?

Before you rush out to order a dozen more packets of Viagra, please remember there are side effects. Priapism, or constant erection, is not so funny. Nor is diarrhea. Do not take on Kol Nidre.

backlash	impact	j-factor	tzurus	kabbalah	good/not good
3.2 +	6.9 x	6	= 60.6 ÷	7 =	8.7

Viagra is GOOD FOR THE JEWS

Vacation Spots

A checklist for traveling Judologists who are unsure about spending their money in countries that do not welcome them.

Country: New Zealand

- Jewish population: 5,000
- Distance from New York: 8,819 miles (14,192 km) (7,663 nautical miles). Flight length: approx. 18.5 hours
- J-Factor: New Zealand has had two Jewish prime ministers: Julius Vogel from 1873 to 1875 and then again in 1876; he was famous for his support of women's suffrage, which led to New Zealand being the first country in the world to give women

the vote, in 1893. Francis Bell was only officially
prime minister for sixteen days in 1925 when
Prime Minister William Massey died. His mother
was Jewish. New Zealand did vote in the UN in
favor of the creation of the State of Israel in 1948.
- Drawback: not much to do when you get there
  other than extreme sports, clearly Not Good for
  the Jews.

New Zealand is a GOOD VACATION SPOT FOR THE JEWS

Country: Malaysia

- Jewish population: 0
- Distance from New York: 9,404 miles (15,134 km)
  (8,172 nautical miles). Flight length: approx. 21
  hours
- J-Factor: Other than the fact that Israelis are not
  allowed into the country, back in October 2003,
  the country's prime minister, Mahathir Mohamad,
  addressed the Tenth Islamic Summit Conference
  with these immortal words:

The Muslims will forever be oppressed and dominated by the Europeans and the Jews . . . 1.3 billion
Muslims cannot be defeated by a few million Jews . . .

The Europeans killed 6 million Jews out of 12 million. But today the Jews rule this world by proxy. They get others to fight and die for them . . . We are up against a people who think. They survived 2000 years of pogroms not by hitting back, but by thinking. They invented and successfully promoted Socialism, Communism, human rights and democracy so that persecuting them would appear to be wrong, so they may enjoy equal rights with others. With these they have now gained control of the most powerful countries and they, this tiny community, have become a world power . . . They are already beginning to make mistakes. And they will make more mistakes. There may be windows of opportunity for us now and in the future. We must seize these opportunities. (source: ADL.org)

Malaysia is NOT A GOOD VACATION SPOT FOR THE JEWS

Country: Guyana

- Jewish population: about 10
- Distance from New York: 2,545 miles (4,096 km) (2,212 nautical miles). Flight length: approx. 5.5 hours
- J-Factor: Guyana had a Jewish president from

1997 to 1999: Janet Jagan, born Janet Rosenberg in Chicago in 1920. She was the first white president of Guyana, the first elected female president in South America, and the first Jewish head of state in South American history. Her son is now entering politics, so there could be another one.

• Drawback: no kosher restaurants.

Guyana is a GOOD VACATION SPOT FOR THE JEWS

Country: Monaco

• Jewish population: Monaco has more Jews per capita than anywhere else in the world bar Israel, at 30.85 per 1,000 people.
• Distance from New York: 4,021 miles (6,471 km) (3,494 nautical miles). Flight length: approx. 8.5 hours
• J-Factor: Jews love a good spiel, so why not go out in style?

Monaco is a GOOD VACATION SPOT FOR JEWS

Country: Iceland

- Jewish population: 12 or so
- Distance from New York: 2,619 miles (4,215 km) (2,276 nautical miles). Flight length: approx. 5.5 hours
- J-Factor: Despite having the smallest self-styled Jewish community in the world, Iceland's first lady is Israeli-born Dorrit Moussaieff, which is quite a feat. With such a small community, why not pop over? What? We're not good enough for you all of a sudden? You never call . . . The community meets for a Seder as well as for Rosh Hashanah and Hanukkah, so now there's no excuse. And yes, Iceland did vote in favor of the creation of the Jewish State.

Iceland is a GOOD VACATION SPOT FOR THE JEWS

Country: Kentucky

- Jewish population: 12,000
- Distance from New York: 653 miles (1,050 km) (567 nautical miles). Flight length: approx. 2.25 hours

- J-Factor: Kentucky's Southern hospitality has not always extended to those of the Hebraic persuasion. In 1862, General Ulysses S. Grant issued an order expelling the Jews from Kentucky for apparently violating trade regulations. (OK, Abe Lincoln commanded him to revoke it three days later, but still.) Despite the Jewish mayor of Louisville (Jerry Abramson), Kentucky is still not a great place for the wandering Judologist. There is an ongoing "debate" about the Christian Right's desire to post the Ten Commandments on every civic building and public school. Some, like State Senator Albert Robinson, believe using the term "Judeo-Christian" is oppressive to Christians, and said we should remember that "when the boat came to these great shores, it did not have an atheist, a Buddhist, a Hindu, a Muslim, a Christian and a Jew. Ninety-eight-plus percent of these people were Christians." (source: religioustolerance.org) It doesn't make you want to rush into putting your kids' names on waiting lists in this state.
- Also, avoid this state in May, for that's when the good ol' Nordic Fest takes place. It's a music festival which is a kind of Woodstock for white supremacists, featuring bands like Race War, Black Shirts, Totenkopf Saints, and Blood and

Iron. This "Newport for the New Right" is run by the Imperial Klans of America (IKA), which believes:

The Imperial Klans of America, Knights of the Ku Klux Klan is a law abiding organization . . . We must protect our race, nation and our great beliefs in Christ . . . The IKA hates: Muds, spics, kikes and niggers. This is our God given right! In no way do we advocate violence. We believe in educating our people to the monopolistic Jewish control of the world's banks, governments and media.

Who could possibly complain about an organization devoted to education?

Kentucky is NOT A GOOD VACATION SPOT FOR THE JEWS

Country: Japan

- Jewish population: 2,000
- Distance from New York: 6,760 miles (10,878 km) (5,874 nautical miles). Flight length: approx. 14 hours
- J-Factor: For a country with so few Jews, there is an impressive amount of anti-Semitic material available to the casual reader, and it sells rather

well. *The Protocols of the Elders of Zion*, *The International Jew*, and *Mein Kampf* all became available in Japanese in the 1920s and 1930s and are published in new editions about every ten years. The main thrust of the anti-Semitism is that Jews' prime concern is world domination as influenced by the *Protocols*. "Jews" is sometimes used as a generic term for "the West." However, this is sophistry. What Jew really enjoys uncooked fish? It's not natural.

Japan is NOT A GOOD VACATION SPOT FOR THE JEWS

Country: Micronesia

Four states: Pohnpei, Yap, Chuuk, and Kosrae, in the Pacific Ocean somewhere between Hawaii and Indonesia

- Jewish population: There were two Baptists in the process of converting to Judaism there, but they've now made aliyah . . . so, none.
- Distance from New York: 7,792 miles (12,539 km) (6,771 nautical miles). Flight length: approx. 35 hours
- J-Factor: Micronesia scores very high on this.

Inexplicably, it has developed such a relationship with Israel that it always votes for Israel at the United Nations. So much so that Yasser Arafat once dubbed Israel "Greater Micronesia." An American Baptist couple, Jim Bramblett and Deborah Greenhill, symbolized this strange link to the Zionist homeland. They lived in Micronesia in a completely kosher house, complete with a mikveh and beit midrash, on a hill known as Mount Zion by locals. They converted to Judaism in Honolulu and now live in Israel, but while they were in Micronesia, they claim, they influenced their government's pro-Israel decisions on such issues as West Bank settlements, nuclear capability, and Palestinian refugees by using the Old Testament to show Micronesian officials that they would be tempting divine retribution if they failed to side with Israel. (source: *Forward*, July 6, 2001)

Micronesia is a GOOD VACATION SPOT FOR THE JEWS

Country: Thailand

- Jewish population: 200
- Distance from New York: 8,664 miles (13,943 km)

(7,529 nautical miles). Flight length: approx. 17 hours

- J-Factor: There are so many Israelis in Thailand (around 50,000 visit each year) that some Thai people working in the tourist areas can actually speak Hebrew. You can visit a kosher restaurant in Bangkok and go for a Friday-night meal on Koh Samui, and if Buddhist temples aren't fulfilling your spiritual needs, Chabad House on the Khao San Road in Bangkok is the place to go for services on Shabbos and festivals, and they even host a free Seder night.

Thailand is a GOOD VACATION SPOT FOR THE JEWS

Country: France

- Jewish population: 600,000
- Distance from New York: 3,635 miles (5,850 km) (3,159 nautical miles). Flight length: approx. 8 hours
- J-Factor: a controversial entry, what with its history of anti-Semitism—Dreyfus, the Vichy government, the recent banning of religious headwear, extreme right-wing politics, and six hundred anti-Semitic attacks in 2004 alone—but what great

food. For Jews, food must be high on the agenda for vacation, and it's madness to ignore the best culinary delights in the world for mere principles.

- The French government does tend to turn a blind eye to events such as the firebombing of synagogues (Lyon, Strasbourg, Marseilles), the Molotov cocktails thrown into a Jewish sports center (Toulouse), the gunman who opened fire in a kosher butcher (Toulouse, again), the numerous desecrations of graveyards and regular defacing of the statue of Dreyfus (Paris), et cetera. The French ambassador to the United Kingdom was heard saying at a dinner party in London that the world's problems were due to "that shitty little country, Israel." President Jacques Chirac proudly scolded a Jewish newspaper editor in January 2005 with the statement that "there is no anti-Semitism in this country."

- It's not all Jew-baiting, though (serious Judologists note that France did vote for the creation of the State of Israel). France did ban the Hizbollah TV station al-Manar for incitement of anti-Semitism, and also has the largest Jewish population in Europe and the third largest in the world, so a show of solidarity would not be out of place. Perhaps the strongest argument to support La Belle France must be its unstinting, unswerving, and unbelievable support of Israel—no other country has voted as consistently highly for Israel in the Eurovision Song Contest.

France is borderline and therefore NOT A GOOD VACATION SPOT FOR THE JEWS

Country: Turkmenistan

- Jewish population: 1,500–2,000
- Distance from New York: 6,241 miles (10,043 km) (5,423 nautical miles). Flight length: don't bother
- J-Factor: President Saparmyrat Niyazov has made himself president for life and rules this state as an absolute dictatorship—so much so that he has even named a yogurt after himself. He has banned ballet, opera, and even the circus. Only two religions are tolerated: Russian Orthodoxy and Sunni Islam. Aside from showing support to the persecuted Jews in this darkest backwater of the old Soviet Empire, *avoid this place*.

Turkmenistan is NOT A GOOD VACATION SPOT FOR THE JEWS

Country: Venezuela

- Jewish population: 35,000
- Distance from New York: 2,120 miles (3,413 km) (1,843 nautical miles). Flight length: approx. 4.75 hours
- J-Factor: According to a report from the Stephen Roth Institute in Tel Aviv University, "In Latin America, and particularly in Venezuela, politicians and high-ranking officials openly express anti-Semitic views." Apparently, during the presidency of Hugo Chávez, the intelligence forces of the Venezuelan police raided a Jewish elementary and high school in the Hebraica Cultural and Sports Club, allegedly in search of arms. The 1,500 children were accused of stashing guns and being behind the assassination of Federal Prosecutor Danilo Anderson. Perhaps the after-school club there is called Mini Mossad? In May 2004, Venezuelan state radio claimed that Jews were disloyal to Venezuela.

Venezuela is NOT A GOOD VACATION SPOT FOR THE JEWS

Country: Bahrain

- Jewish population: about 30
- Distance from New York: 6,628 miles (10,667 km) (5,760 nautical miles). Flight time: approx. 17 hours
- J-Factor: Of all the Arab states, Bahrain is interesting because of its ambiguous stance toward Israel and the Jews. Aside from Egypt and Jordan, which are at peace with Israel, most other Arab nations will not allow Jews across their borders if they have the stamp of Israel on their passports. Bahrain, however, has entertained peace talks with Israel, and Bahraini Jews and Bahrainis enjoy seminormal relationships. Before the creation of Israel in 1948, six hundred Jews lived in Bahrain. Today only thirty Jews live in Bahrain, but the Jewish community is on the rise and is tolerated. Even the U.S. State Department has released a report complimenting Bahrain's policy of religious tolerance. The report, which examined religious tolerance throughout the world, noted that Bahrain's constitution provided for freedom of worship for both Muslims and non-Muslims. It may not be Miami Beach, but if you want to dip

your toe in the Arab world, this Gulf State might be the place to start.

Bahrain is a GOOD VACATION SPOT FOR THE JEWS

Country: Honduras

- Jewish population: about 200
- Distance from New York: 2,000 miles (3,218 km) (1,738 nautical miles). Flight length: approx. 4.5 hours
- J-Factor: Despite abstaining in the UN vote over the creation of the State of Israel, Honduras has had two Jewish presidents: Juan Lindo, president from 1847 to 1852; and Ricardo Maduro (born April 20, 1946, in Panama), who became president in 2002 despite a constitutional ban on non-Honduran-born presidents. Apart from Marranos (descendants of the Jews who were expelled from Spain in 1492 and practiced in secret), who came to Honduras and assimilated completely, Jews first arrived at the end of the nineteenth century and were welcomed to the country throughout the 1920s until 1936, when immigration was halted. In the last fifteen years there has been a resurgence of Jewish life, and there is a private Jewish ceme-

tery as well as a Jewish burial society. Shul membership fees are very reasonable, so it's well worth contemplating a share in a condo here.

Honduras is a GOOD VACATION SPOT FOR THE JEWS

Country: England

- Jewish population: 250,000
- Distance from New York: 3,470 miles (5,585 km) (3,016 nautical miles). Flight time: approx. 6.75 hours
- J-Factor: Tony Blair's close relationship with George Bush has not always meant he shares the president's upbeat analysis of Israel's innocence in all things Middle Eastern. Prime Minister Blair's failed Roadmap to Peace initiative does not mean he will give up meddling. Traditionally, the left in Britain has supported Israel, but post-1967 the shift was quite dramatically reversed. The media, including the world-famous BBC, has often been criticized by Jews as being anti-Israel, but on the whole, good old-fashioned anti-Semitism exists in such a polite form that Judologists should not be put off seeing the Motherland and enjoying a cup of tea at Fortnum & Mason, London's poshest delicatessen.

- A famous story of an American visiting Fortnum's goes like this: "Hey, boy, gimme a pound of lox," the American orders the assistant. "By that, I understand you to mean smoked salmon, and here is your appropriate quantity." "Actually, make that chopped liver, too," the American continues. "By that, I understand you to mean pâté de foie gras, and here is your dish." "One last thing," the American ventures. "Please deliver the whole lot and a dozen blintzes to the Ritz Hotel next Saturday." "By that I understand you to mean crepes, and I'm afraid we don't deliver on Shabbos."
- The British Jewish community boasts the world's oldest Jewish newspaper, the *Jewish Chronicle*, founded in 1841, which provides an invaluable service to British Jews with its famous classifieds section providing weekly lists of the dead, the born, and the married. It is a wonderful reminder of who you have fallen out with and why.

England is a GOOD VACATION SPOT FOR THE JEWS

Country: Kazakhstan

- Jewish population: 15,000–20,000
- Distance from New York: 6,367 (10,245 km) (5,533

nautical miles). Flight length: approx. 15 hours.

- J-Factor: The former Soviet republic has a questionable reputation when it comes to anti-Semitism due in part to the activities of Borat Sagdiyev, the fictional creation of comic actor Sacha Baron Cohen. The Kazakh government threatened the actor with a legal suit in 2005 because it found his portrayal of Kazakhs derogatory and inflammatory. In fact, so angry were Kazakhs about some of the "inaccuracies" in Mr. Baron Cohen's depiction of their country, the government took out a four-page ad in the *New York Times* to argue that: the national drink is, in fact, kumiss (horse milk) and not horse piss, as claimed by Cohen's alter ego, Borat; most women are not kept in cages; and there is no evidence of a Kazakh folk song called "Throw Jews Down a Well."

- Borat has distanced himself from Mr. Baron Cohen, declaring on his Web site, www.borat.tv, "I fully support my government's position to sue the Jew." He goes further, adding that "Kazakhstan is as civilised as any other country in the world. Women can now travel on inside of bus, homosexuals no longer have to wear blue hat and age of consent has been raised to 8 years old."

- Kazakhstan enjoys an integrated ethnic

population and has a cordial relationship with Israel (in fact, in 2004 more than $300 million was invested in the country from Israel). Be aware, though, of the "orteke" dance, as it enacts the pain felt by a goat falling into a hole. Don't laugh when you see this in a Kazakstani tavern as this is a cultural tradition.

- Oh, yes—Kazakhstan is one of the top oil producers in the world (currently ranked 13). So, stock up while you are there.

Kazakhstan is a GOOD VACATION SPOT FOR THE JEWS

(Sources: Stephen Roth Institute and ADL.org)

1492

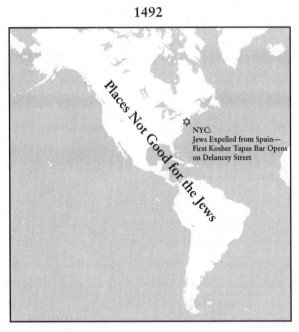

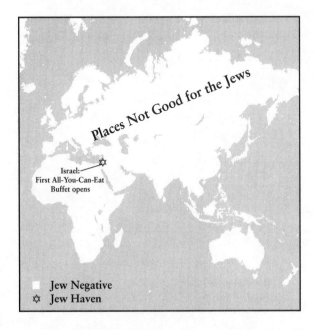

1897

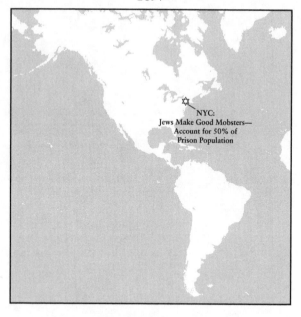

NYC:
Jews Make Good Mobsters—
Account for 50% of
Prison Population

Places (Still) Not Good for the Jews

Israel:
First Zionist Congress:
Jews Shout at Each Other.
Again.

■ Jew Negative
☆ Jew Haven

2006

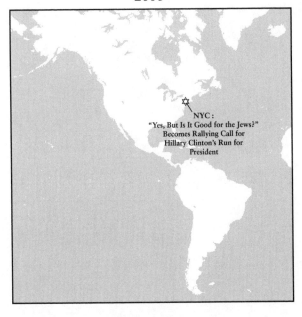

NYC :
"Yes, But Is It Good for the Jews?"
Becomes Rallying Call for
Hillary Clinton's Run for
President

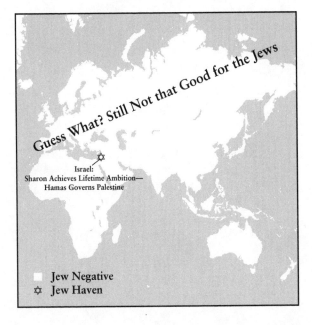

Guess What? Still Not that Good for the Jews

Israel:
Sharon Achieves Lifetime Ambition—
Hamas Governs Palestine

☆ Jew Negative
☆ Jew Haven

Webber, Andrew Lloyd, musicals of (born March 22, 1948, in London) Arguably the most popular and successful British composer of musical theater of the late twentieth century, with multiple musicals that have run for more than a decade both on Broadway and in the West End. In 2005, Lloyd Webber sold four of the twelve West End theaters he has 50 percent stakes in to Broadway producers Max Weitzenhoffer and Nica Burns.

Joseph and the Amazing Technicolor Dreamcoat was the first musical theater show written by the team of Andrew Lloyd Webber and Tim Rice. This musical retelling of the Joseph story is undoubtedly positive for the Jews and includes the following advice to Joseph from Pharaoh: "Find a man to lead you through the famine / With a flair for economic planning"—which inspired a generation of accountants.

It is not this sympathetic rags-to-riches rendering of how the first Jew became CFO of Egypt but Lloyd Webber's second work, *Jesus Christ Superstar*, that presents possible areas of concern for the Judologist. Clearly, any depiction of Judas Iscariot in mainstream culture is not great for the Jews. And do they have to go on about it? Eight performances a week, all over the world. It was 2,000 years ago . . .

The final nail in the coffin for the richest composer in the world must be one of his biggest successes, 1981's *Cats*. The lyrics were based on T. S. Eliot's 1939 *Old Possum's Book of Practical Cats*, which Lloyd Webber confessed was a childhood favorite. Before January 9, 2006, when *Phantom of the Opera* took over the mantle, *Cats* had been the longest-running Broadway musical, spanning a reign of more than twenty years. T. S. Eliot was a notorious anti-Semite who famously said in a lecture at the University of Virginia in 1933: "Reasons of race and religion combine to make any large number of free-thinking Jews undesirable." There is also the famous line in Eliot's poem of 1920 "Burbank with a Baedeker: Bleistein with a cigar," which compares Jews to rats. Mmmm.

backlash   impact   j-factor   tzurus   kabbalah   good/not good

$$4 \quad + \quad 4 \quad \times \quad 1 \quad = \quad 8 \quad \div \quad 7 \quad = \quad 1.14$$

The musicals of Andrew Lloyd Webber are NOT GOOD FOR THE JEWS

Wimbledon Tennis Championships An annual event that lasts for two weeks every June in the borough of Merton in South West London (population 38,192). The tournament went from a small "garden party" gathering in 1877 with a few hundred onlookers to the most important lawn tennis competition in the world, with over 500,000 international visitors plus millions of viewers on television. Not to be confused with Wimbledon, North Dakota (population 275).

The All England Lawn Tennis Club, the organization that runs the tournament, has not always been as inclusive an institution as its title proclaims.

When Brit Angela Buxton won the Wimbledon Doubles Championship of 1956 with American Althea Gibson, their victory did not result in the traditional invitation to join the exclusive All England Club. Perhaps their forehand lobs were not developed enough for inclusion on the prestigious membership list? Or could it be because they were Jewish and black?

Ms. Buxton, not one to hold a long-term broygus, declared in a recent interview with the *New York Post* (June 13, 2004): "I think the anti-Semitism is still there." Understandable though, as the fiftieth anniversary of the snub approached and she still had not been invited to become a member of the club.

But the most recent example of the uneasy relationship

between tennis and the Jews came in May 2005, during the Qatar Total German Open Tennis Tournament (yes, it had to be in Germany). An article in the annual program featured nostalgic photos of Hermann Goering at Berlin's Rot-Weiss Club and described the club's "golden age" as having occurred during the Juden Frei years. Oh, Happy Days.

On a brighter note, there have been some Jewish success stories at Wimbledon. Dick Savitt was the first Jewish champion, winning the men's singles title in 1951 (although he did beat fellow Jew Herb Flam in the semis, which is a bit of a shame).

Several other Jewish tennis players have competed at Wimbledon (Jonathan Erlich, Brian Gottfried, Pierre Darmon, Anna Smashnova, and others) but Richard Raskin (a.k.a. Renee Richards) must win the prize for being the most versatile, having played in both the men's and women's pro tours. Yes, Richard "swings both ways." Raskin underwent a sex-change operation, and the New York Supreme Court granted her the right to play in the women's tour in 1977. Renee Richards returned to opthalmology after her tennis career ended. Much more sensible job for a nice Jewish boy, I mean girl.

backlash		impact		j-factor		tzurus	kabbalah		good/not good
2.2	+	4.5	x	2.1	= 14.07 ÷	7		=	2.01

Wimbledon is NOT GOOD FOR THE JEWS

Windsor, Henry (Prince Harry of England) (born September 15, 1984, in London) Prince Henry—always known as Prince Harry—is third in line of succession to the British throne, behind his father, the Prince of Wales, and his elder brother, Prince William. In September 1998, Harry started at Eton College, Windsor, passing two A-level exams: Art (scoring a B) and Geography (scoring a D). Prince Harry then left England to spend the first part of his year off before college in Australia and then went to Africa, where he worked in an orphanage in Lesotho. In May 2005, Prince Harry entered the Royal Military Academy Sandhurst to begin his training as an officer in the Army. On July 5, 2005, Prince Harry was cleared of cheating on his Art A-level.

On January 8, 2005, Harry attended a "fancy-dress" costume party on the theme of "colonials and natives" at a country estate in Wiltshire. Mmm . . . what could the third in line to the throne of England wear? Ceremonial robes from an old family wardrobe? Something from the Tudors, perhaps? Oh, I know, a MILITARY TUNIC with a GERMAN FLAG on the arm and a SWASTIKA armband.

Now, fancy-dress parties can be clear indicators of subconscious activity, and it must be considered of the utmost gravity when a member of the British royal family enjoys his Saturday night kitted out as a member of the Wehrmacht.

However, the timing of this outrageous act of poor taste

was perfect for the Jewish community—two weeks later, the British commemoration of the sixtieth anniversary of the liberation of the Auschwitz was due to take place and otherwise might have gone unnoticed, were it not for the furor created by Prince Harry's whimsical choice of outfit. This must surely be seen as a good act for the Jews? However, his choice to take his year off in Australia and Lesotho and not on a kibbutz in northern Israel must be viewed dimly. As there is some question over his paternity, an unusually high J-Factor for a royal will be calculated.

backlash	impact	j-factor	tzurus	kabbalah	good/bad
6.8	+ 5.22	x 1.79	= 21.52	÷ 7	= 3.07

Prince Harry is NOT GOOD FOR THE JEWS

Xmas Christmas is the Christian festival that falls on December 25 and celebrates the birth of Jesus. It is generally accepted that Jesus was not actually born on this day, and some theologians believe the festival was established at this time of year to coincide with the pagan winter solstice, thereby encouraging pagans to accept Christ as the Lord.

A happy time for most people, Xmas is also hugely important to the health of a nation's economy. Most retailers develop their whole marketing strategy around the period before Xmas, and profits are dictated by customer spending in the gift-purchasing period from Thanksgiving to Xmas.

Hollywood is also geared to this festive season. Interestingly, as Tom Teicholz pointed out in the *Jewish Journal of Los Angeles*, many seasonal blockbusters have been conceived and produced by Jews. *Elf* (2004), directed, written, and starred in by Jews (Jon Favreau, David Berenbaum, James Caan, Edward Asner), grossed over $150 million. Perhaps the most famous Jewish Xmas movie is *White Christmas* (1954, Michael Curtiz, Norm Krasna, and Danny Kaye). Only fitting really, considering it is a celebration of the World's Most Famous Jew.

Christmas is also a good time for Jewish identity. To be able to say boldly to work colleagues "Oh, I'm not doing anything for Christmas. I'm Jewish" often wins gasps of admiration, loathing, and slight envy—a reaction most Jews are used to by now.

The commercialization of Christmas has led to the commercialization of Hanukkah—not a good thing for Jews. Don't forget, Jews have to buy eight presents for the eight days of the festival. No longer can a parent get away with a doughnut and $1 bill, but there are only so many PlayStation III games a Jew can afford. Mind you, we should spare a thought for those poor followers of Jews for Jesus who get hit for both holidays. Ouch.

This commercialization of religion does come at a price: A Jewish turkey farmer goes to the Vatican and promises a donation of $50 million if the pope will change the Lord's Prayer to "Give us this day our daily turkey." The pope refuses. The turkey farmer raises the offer to $75 million. Still no. Finally, he leaves an offer of $100 million on the table. The next day, the pope announces to the Vatican Assembly some good news and some bad news. "Good news: we have received $100 million from an anonymous donor. Bad news: we have lost the Wonderloaf account."

Perhaps the best description of Jews' experience at Xmas is movingly portrayed in the classic song "The Lonely Jew on Christmas" (*South Park*). In the *Judology Quarterly Review*, Solomon Pinkas wrote of the lyric, "An excoriating critique of Christmas as seen by a young Jewish boy. Each year, while his chimney goes ignored, the boy is stuck lighting candles, night after night, and forced to suffer the indignaties of eating kosher latkes instead of traditional hams. A devastating exploration of the true Hebrew condition at Christmas—the Jew is reduced to loneliness and self-absorption" (*JQR*, 2006, Paranoid Publications).

backlash		*impact*		*j-factor*		*tzurus*		*kabbalah*		*good/not good*
5.2	+	6.8	x	6.1	= 73.2	÷	7		=	10.4

Xmas is GOOD FOR THE JEWS

Yes, But Is It Good for the Jews? First published by Bloomsbury in 2006, this beginner's guide revealed the secrets of Judology to the unsuspecting public. The determination of whether something or somebody is Good for the Jews caused some controversy, and the book was publicly burned in parts of New York and not stocked in several bookshops for fear of reprisals. This was later to be revealed as a publicity stunt.

Bloomsbury USA and Penguin UK, the publishing companies behind this book, do, remarkably, employ non-Jews, which proves that there is diversity in publishing, as opposed to Hollywood. The acquiring editors involved with this edition are not Jews (they're Roman Catholic and Church of England), therefore cannot be blamed for publishing this book, which some have already described as "cynical religious pornography" (*Der Yiddisher Tam-Tam*, Paris, 2006).

"Yes, but is it good for the Jews?" is a common phrase used even among non-Jews. Corporate executives, for example, have been heard to ponder the wisdom of certain strategic decisions with the question: Yes, but is it good for the Jews? In other words, is it going to suit our narrow, focused goals and will it do us harm? For the semioticians among you, the phrase is code for "Let's face it, everyone is out to get us, so before proceeding, let's check if this is going to play badly for us."

Judology is a pseudoscience with no explanation of how the scoring is determined, which renders the entire exercise highly dubious. Rumors have floated on the Internet that the author is a member of the extreme right JANGFY movement (Jews Are Not Good for You) which went underground after the first edition of *Yes, but* outsold *The Da Vinci Code* two to one in its first week on the shelves. The publishers simply refer to the author, whom they've never met, as "Deep Jew."

Is this concept a narrow-minded and parochial view from a paranoid people that typifies all that is wrong with modern-day Jews? Or is it a necessary reminder that Jews must be on guard at all times to detect danger in everyday life? Either way, do you have to shout about it so?

You decide.

backlash   *impact*   *j-factor*   *tzurus*   *kabbalah*   *good/not good*

? + ? x ? = ? ÷ 7 = ?

Yes, But is it Good for the Jews? *is* _____

Zoolatry Put simply, the worship of one's pet animal(s).

Jews are prohibited from walking their dogs on the Sabbath or pulling them on leashes on the day of rest, so it is not surprising that traditionally, Jews have not been huge dog owners. Who needs the mishegoss of jerking little Rover to shul? Also, there is a law that does not allow adults to eat before their dog has. Enough said? (Forget Shabbos, what about Yom Kippur? Rover hasn't had to stay in shul all day breathing in everyone else's halitosis.)

Under Jewish law, dogs have the same rights as humans and therefore are commanded to rest on Sabbath and holy days. No switching channels as Shabbos Goy (or dog).

Jews might not have pets (frumer Jews have lots of children, which amounts to the same thing), but Jewish law and tradition look very kindly on animals. In fact, unlike Christianity and most civilizations until 1800, Judaism has always outlawed cruelty to animals. Remember, Jacob, Moses, and David were all shepherds; in fact, Moses got his job as leader of the Jews because of his skill in caring for animals—"Since you are merciful to the flock of a human being, you shall be the shepherd of My flock, Israel" (the Talmud).

Jews and dogs go back a long way. There is a midrash (Tanchumah), according to pupsforpeace.org, that tells the rather gruesome story of what happened after the Red Sea drowned the duped Egyptians: "Each Jew took his dog, and went to the body of an Egyptian, putting his foot on the Egyptians throat. He then said to his dog, 'Eat the hand that enslaved me!' Thus, the Jews had dogs, and they left in the Exodus along with the Jews."

This blind love of the pet can go too far—for example, the recent phenomenon of the "bark mitzvah." A rabbi starts with the blessing said when seeing beautiful animals and ends the ceremony by awarding a bark mitzvah certificate to the dog's owner. I suppose an Arts Scroll Series is a step too far.

Kindness to animals has extended to the Middle Eastern conflict. In 2005, after the withdrawal from Gaza, many pets were left in the ruined former settlers' residencies. Tali Lavie, a spokesperson for Hakol Chai (an animal-related legislation lobby group), says Israelis believe the pets are brave "disengagement dogs." A similar sentiment has often been expressed by the Palestinian leadership, except perhaps omitting the word "brave" and referring to their owners.

backlash   impact   j-factor   tzurus   kabbalah   good/not good

4.4   +   3.5   x   6.8   = 53.72 ÷   7   =   7.67

Zoolatry is borderline and therefore NOT GOOD FOR THE JEWS

Acknowledgments

First, I would like to thank my wife, Karen, for her love, support, and unstinting belief in this project, but I can't — she was dead against it.

On a lighter note, I am indebted to the Great Karen Rinaldi and all at Bloomsbury for taking the risk on this book, and especially the brilliant Yelena "kosher tattoo" Gitlin and Colin "three out of four" Dickerman for their advice, belief, and expertise. Many thanks to Helen Conford and all the team at Penguin Press too. Special thanks to Claire "research is my middle name" Berliner for her brilliance, and cheers to all my colleagues at Curtis Brown (Viv Schuster, Doug Kean, and Alice Lutyens especially) who tolerated the repeated printing of this manuscript on company time. Thank-you to Anna Davis, who took the poisoned chalice of representing me and taught an old dog some tricks. A special thanks to all of the authors I represent—for turning a blind eye to this strange project.

As with all Jewish families, I owe most of the material in this book to mine. They may not have known it, but I learned to view everything from the fall of Margaret Thatcher to the price of apples in terms of whether it was good or not for the Jews. Their humor, love, and support have allowed me to bring their name into such disrepute with this book, and for that I thank the Gellers, Mum, Dad, Phil, and Rich. Special thanks must go to Andrew Mattison, the source of some fantastic jokes (and dreadful ones too) and to Charlotte Mendelson, Claire Tisne, Geoff Kloske, Bruce Tracy, David Hirshey, Greg Williams, Richard Charkin and Toby Mundy for early enthusiasm.

My family of friends that began with Habonim all those years ago must be thanked, as those late-night debates about whether gefilte fish did in fact improve sperm counts proved invaluable; so a big thank-you to Marshall Yarm, Adam Goldwater, Jonny Mendelson, Jonny Gould, and all who contributed in some way to this book. Jonny Marks and Jonny Freedland are more Jonnys who deserve my gratitude. Marks is a number one mensch/friend and Freedland is a great mentor and fantastic friend and I hope he enjoyed seeing his consigliere turning to him for advice for once.

Oh, all right, Karen, thank-you, doll.

A Note on the Author

Jonny Geller is the director of the Judological Institute of Spiritual Mathematics whose international headquarters is in Cockfosters.

The
Godmother
Tree

The Godmother Tree

Ruth Wallace-Brodeur

A Charlotte Zolotow Book
An Imprint of HarperCollins*Publishers*

The Godmother Tree
Copyright © 1988 by Ruth Wallace-Brodeur
First published by Vermont Migrant Education Program
ica. For information address HarperCollins Children's Books, a division of
HarperCollins Publishers, 10 East 53rd Street, New York, NY 10022.
Typography by Joyce Hopkins
1 2 3 4 5 6 7 8 9 10
First HarperCollins Edition, 1992

Library of Congress Cataloging-in-Publication Data
Wallace-Brodeur, Ruth.
    The godmother tree / Ruth Wallace Brodeur. —New ed.
        p.   cm.
    "A Charlotte Zolotow book."
    Summary: When ten-year-old Laura moves with her family to yet another new
farm, Laura slowly begins to build connections to the place, to her family, and to
herself.
    ISBN 0-06-022457-6. —ISBN 0-06-022458-4 (lib. bdg.)
    [1. Moving, Household—Fiction. 2. Farm life—Fiction.] I. Title.
PZ7.W15883Go 1992   91–17951
[Fic]—dc20   CIP
                                                                        AC

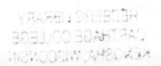

For my father,
Emery Lincoln Wallace

*With my thanks to Robin Ulmer,
Michael Campbell, and the Barrows family*

CHAPTER

1

WEDNESDAY, LAST WEEK of school in June. Laura had lost track of the date in the confusion of the past few days. Monday she was mending her blue shorts to wear to fifth-grade field day, and on Tuesday, instead of running the 100-yard dash, she was packing those shorts into the red duffel bag Gramma Ryan had given her and moving clear across the county to Redfield. She packed the duffel herself and held it on her lap the whole way, because the last time they moved she lost her marble collection and autograph book, among other things that didn't matter so much.

"Must have got left with that stuff I set aside for Family Relief," Mama had said, and of course they couldn't go back for it, not after the fight Daddy had with Mr. Tuttle. Tipsy Tuttle, they called him, as he was drunk more often than not. That was the reason for the fight. Daddy told old Tipsy his farm was washing right down the gutter on a tide of alcohol, and Tipsy told Daddy to clear out by dawn the next day. They hadn't been gone by dawn, but they were by noon.

This time there wasn't any fight. Daddy had been working double at the Blairs' ever since the other hand was laid up with a broken pelvis. When he hadn't had a day off in two months and no extra pay to show for it, Daddy was watching the ads and keeping his ears open. Sunday Uncle Ed had come by and said Ralph Turner over in Redfield was looking for somebody real quick. Daddy went over after chores and came back saying the deal was a sight better than they were getting at the Blairs', and here they were, last week of school, starting at a new place. Mama said now maybe

2

she could get a decent night's rest; she was convinced their trailer at the Blairs' was a death trap just waiting to roar into flames.

Luther didn't say much; he never did. Starting new at school again didn't worry him any. Laura knew he didn't plan to go back to school in the fall now he was sixteen, no matter what Mama said about the value of an education. Ryan pulled a major sulk, which in Laura's opinion wasn't all that different from his usual behavior at home. Ryan could charm anybody into his fan club in three seconds flat, but it wasn't a talent he wasted on his family. He'd barely talked to any of them since he'd heard about the move, though Mama kept at him with little bribes and treats. Ryan didn't care if their trailer exploded or Daddy never got time off as long as he could play baseball. At Blairs', Ryan was the star of the Ridgeview Central School team and had planned to play summer league.

If they had to move again, Laura was glad it was at the end of the school year, though she wished they could have waited until after field day. She had been practicing along the road by their trailer every night till she was almost

3

sure she could win the sprints. If Peter Cook came through on the jumps, their class had a good chance to win the watermelon.

Laura had hoped she and Ryan could wait until fall to start at Redfield Middle School. She begged Mama to let her stay home on Wednesday and help get things settled, but Mama was certain it would be easier if they met some people right off. So there Laura was, sitting in Room 22 of Redfield Middle School just seventeen hours after moving to town, watching kids put away books, clean out desks, and take their art off the walls. She wondered what Mr. Blackburn would do with the picture she'd drawn of a frog pond at night. It was hanging on the wall over the fish tank at Ridgeview—now she'd never get it back.

Mr. Blackburn had been a pretty good teacher; better than this one seemed, anyway. She'd *tsk*ed and sighed and gotten all frowny at having to deal with Laura at this point in the school year. She finally parked her over by the empty bookshelves with two sick plants to stare at. Laura could see the problem: tiny white bugs lined every vein of the pale limp leaves, probably sucking the life juices right out of them.

The teacher looked like a similar sort of thing was eating at her. She had pale hair, pale skin, and a pale voice that everybody ignored.

"No one is leaving this room until every scrap is where it belongs," the voice repeated in the background like a damaged record, but the room was still littered with papers, books, and apple cores when the bell rang for the kids to visit their next year's classrooms. Laura didn't know whether to follow them out the door with no idea where to go or to stay with the sick plants while a new group scrambled for seats in the mess.

"Everybody find a desk, any desk for now." The teacher was stuck in a new groove before she noticed Laura still sitting by the bookshelves. "No, no, dear." She sighed and closed her eyes, struggling to hang in there. "This is Move-Up Day. You won't be in this room next year."

"Where will I be?" Laura asked.

The voice broke loose. "*I* don't know these things. *I* don't make out the schedules. If they didn't tell you at the office, you'll have to go back and ask. Now, everybody find a desk, any desk for now."

"Come on, Riley," Laura muttered without moving her lips. She'd turned to Riley at times like this ever since that perfect Sunday they'd spent last summer at Crystal Lake. Daddy and Luther and Mama's friend Cindy had all been there. Laura had a new bathing suit, there was barbecued chicken and Laura's favorite green apples for lunch, and the girl at the next picnic table very obviously wanted to play. "This is the life of Riley," Cindy announced as she stretched out on her beach towel with a can of lemonade and her transistor radio. From then on, Riley was everything right to Laura. She felt better talking to her, the same way she felt better just writing Mama's name on all those letters she'd sent home the time she thought she'd die of homesickness at the rural education camp.

Laura picked her way out of the room and went back along the hall to the office. She stood in front of a long counter lined with neat stacks of papers. The woman who had told them where to go earlier, when Mama brought her and Ryan in, collected a sheet from each pile and stapled the packet together with a bang at the end of the row. After four tours along the course, she paused.

"Yes?" she asked without looking up. "What is it?"

"I don't know where to go for next year's class," Laura said to the woman's green eyelids.

"Didn't your teacher give you a packet with that information in it?" The lady was starting back along the row.

"No," Laura said.

"Well, who's your teacher?"

"I don't know. I just came here this morning and you said go to Room 22."

The woman stopped and finally looked at Laura. "Oh, yes," she remembered. "You're the farm kid. What was your name again?"

"Laura Cate."

The woman finished another set of papers, then went to the desk against the back wall. "Laura Cate. Yes, that's right," she said, as though Laura's answer checked with a correction sheet at the back of her big red book. "Well, Laura, I can't give you your math and reading sections as we have no records on you as yet, but I will assign you to . . ." She flipped through several pages, tracing and tapping on each one with long red nails. "To Miss Dunbar's class for now. That's Room 36. It's up the stairs and along to the right. I'd take you myself, but I'm minding the store alone here today."

"Thank you," Laura said. "I can find it.

"We'll look in the fall, Riley, if we're still here." Laura went down the steps and out into the sun. She'd wait in the park across the street until it was time to find her bus. Number 6, Mama had said. Her last two bus routes, at Tuttles' and Blairs', had been Number 3. When she'd first started school, she'd taken the C bus. "C for Cate, Laura, isn't that nice?" Mama had said as though the school had arranged it just for her. That was when they lived at Hastingses' farm. Laura remembered standing at the top of the big steps of the C bus when it stopped at their mailbox, watching in terror as the door swung back to see if Mrs. Hastings's awful goose was waiting to chase her. That goose had been run over by a car two weeks before the Hastingses auctioned off their herd and the Cates moved to Tuttles'. It was the only two weeks Laura didn't feel sick going home on the C bus.

Laura felt the familiar squeezing start in her chest as she watched four buses pull up in front of the Redfield school. Mama must have gotten the number wrong. Then her breathing steadied. Only four buses, but the one at the back of the line had a big 6 by the door. "Be sure to tell the driver to stop at the corner of Valley Road," Mama had said. "He's not going to know you or where you belong." Laura would make Ryan tell the driver. If he wouldn't, they'd stay on there until the last stop and pretend that was the one they wanted. She'd make Ryan sit with her, too, even though he probably had a million friends already and wouldn't think it was cool for an almost eighth grader to sit with his sister. She'd make him sit on the aisle seat so she could look out the window and not at the other kids. It wouldn't be long now; this was just half a day. And tomorrow she wouldn't have to come at all. Mama said so, as they were just giving out report cards and stuff like that. Mama would want to know who she had for next year. Laura would tell her Miss Dunbar and, yes, she was probably very nice. Mama would smile and say, "See? That wasn't so bad," and feel good that once again they'd made a new start.

2

WHEN THEIR BLUE CHEVY had pulled up to the big white farmhouse on Valley Road, Laura at first thought Daddy was stopping to ask for more water to pour in their steaming radiator. But when Mama heaved herself out of the front seat and started up the walk after him, Laura crawled out from the cartons and bags stacked around her. She stood twisting a strand of her long brown hair around and around her finger the way she did when she was uncertain. This must be Turners' farm, then. The front porch drooped and the paint was peeling, but a maple spread its fresh green canopy over the front yard, and a well-kept barn with a round turret was just across the road. Laura couldn't see where they would be living; she hoped it wasn't too far, so Daddy could come in for coffee or lunch breaks.

"Grab a load and come on, girl," Mama said as she came back and lowered the creaking tailgate.

"Here?" Laura barely got her arms out in time to catch the box of dishes Mama was handing her. "We're going to live here?" She couldn't believe it. They'd only lived in one house that she could remember, and then not a two-story one, or one with a porch, or one anywhere near this big.

"Is it all ours?" she asked Daddy as he anchored the door open. "Where do the Turners live?"

"Up the road and over that rise a piece," he said. "The other hand, man name of Granger, lives on that end there." Daddy pointed to an ell that extended back from the south end of the house. "What do you think? Some better than we come from, I guess." Daniel Cate looked about with satisfaction, while his wife struggled with another load.

"Will you two lend a hand?" she puffed in irritation, but just then Luther and Ryan rattled up in Uncle Ed's truck with the rest of their stuff bulging in back.

"Can you believe it?" Laura danced up to the cab. "This is *it*, this whole house is *ours*, except for that little part on the end. It even has a porch and maybe we get to have our own rooms."

"Looks big enough, that's for sure." Luther smiled at Laura's excitement, but Ryan was careful to show no interest. Laura bet he hadn't said one word the whole way, when she'd been dying to ride in the truck with Luther. But Mama said, "No, the boys will take the truck and you ride with us, Laura." Mama had a thing about brothers facing the world together. She didn't seem to notice that it killed Ryan to be seen with any of them, including Luther, unless maybe they could drive around all dolled up in a Cadillac with not one thing to show they were from a farm.

"Come on, come on," Mama yelled from the car. "Let's get this stuff in the house. The place is a hog pen, but with a little elbow grease . . ."

When she saw the inside of the kitchen,

Laura figured one more drop of any kind of grease and the whole thing would slide off down the road. But the house had even more room than it looked from the outside, with a bedroom for everybody and some left over. Mama and Daddy put their things in one of the back rooms downstairs, while Ryan grabbed the other as though it were first prize. Luther and Laura were left with their choice of the big rooms upstairs. Laura picked a front room with tall windows that looked across the fields to Lake Champlain and the Adirondack Mountains beyond, and Luther set his bag in a room across the hall that got the morning sun.

"You'll roast in summer and freeze in winter," Mama fretted. "It will be a miracle if you don't fall down those stairs trying to find the bathroom at night." Mama liked to identify the booby traps of a new place right off. If anyone else complained, she immediately started listing reasons why it was the best thing that had ever happened to them.

Laura didn't sleep much that first night, worrying about school the next day. When she did fall asleep, she had a nightmare that a tidal wave was coming and everybody was running away up the steep hill behind their trailer at the Blairs'. She tried to keep up, but her legs dragged like a stuffed doll's. The people were almost out of sight. . . .The wave roared closer behind. . . .

Laura woke up trembling and sweating in the pitch dark. The black space felt endless one minute and like a tight box the next, as though the walls she couldn't see were opening and shutting around her like the flip-up lid on Mama's teakettle. She lay rigid, clutching the edge of her blanket until the windows grayed in the coming dawn enough for her to make out the shape of the big room, empty except for her mattress.

"Luther says it sounded like you had a nightmare last night," Mama said at breakfast, and when Laura got home from school that first-last day, she found Mama's favorite blue china lamp standing on the floor by her mattress.

Laura took off her school clothes and collapsed on the bed. She pulled her yellow blanket over her head, trying to forget the sound of whispers and giggles as she and Ryan had lurched up the aisle to tell the bus driver where

15

to stop. "It's over for this year, Riley," she whispered. She had the whole long summer before she'd have to worry about Redfield Middle School again.

Laura unwrapped the blanket and looked around her room. Although it was true that the same things that had stuffed their trailer to the choking point now looked naked and alone in all this space, she didn't mind the bareness the way Mama seemed to. She'd slept in a utility closet at Blairs', and before that she'd always shared a room with Luther and Ryan. Even without the view, this room could be beautiful. She would pull off those strips of loose wallpaper and then tack up pictures to cover the stains and rough places. Luther had a big roll of newsprint he used to draw on before he started working with Daddy. Maybe he'd have time here to help her make something really good.

As it turned out, there was no time for anyone to draw pictures that first week in Redfield. Laura had forgotten the frenzy Mama got into trying to fix up a new place, working herself and everybody else to pieces until she finally gave up in a flood of tears. They started as usual with the kitchen, scrubbing the stove and the counters, the floor, the windows, and the greasy walls.

"I count five different wallpapers," Mama said in disgust, "all held up in the corners with tape. It's a wonder we haven't been buried alive. Just keep stripping that loose stuff, Ryan, till you get down to something solid."

"Imagine letting a house like this go to ruin." The twist of her screwdriver emphasized each word as Mama tightened the hinges on the porch door. "This place could be right out of a picture postcard, but here our bedroom smells like something died in the walls, and I've never seen such flies. There's not a decent screen anywhere."

The tearful surrender finally came one afternoon as Mama and Laura were trying to scrape what looked like a melted plastic plate off the living-room floor. "That's it, that's all I can do, Laura." Mama sat back as tears began to polish the fine freckles on her round cheeks and splash down to stain her faded blue blouse. "The rest is up to Turner, and I never met a boss yet who bothered to look beyond the barn to the house." She looked around at the cracked walls, the tall windows, the bare old floorboards. "Well, at least it's clean. I wouldn't have done this much if it weren't for Gramma Ryan. For the first time since I was married, I got the space for her to stay. Do you know she's never spent one single night with us?"

Laura patted her mother's shoulder, relieved that the frantic cleaning seemed to be over for this time. She was the only one left helping. Ryan had deserted long ago with a string of fake excuses, and Daddy and Luther were busy with the farm.

"I'll tell you, Laura"—and now Mama's tears came faster—"even though I hated that trailer and never seeing your father or the money to make up for it, I still mind leaving Cindy. I don't make friends like that every day." Mama blew her nose on the cleaning rag. "And I can't bear to think what leaving all your school friends again is doing to you kids."

"I don't mind, Mama," Laura said truthfully, for even though she didn't like starting a new school, she didn't much mind leaving an old one anymore. She usually made friends, but not anyone special, not someone to come for supper or to sleep over. Either the Cates didn't have the room or they lived too far out or other

18

parents didn't know Laura's well enough to feel comfortable dropping their kids off. No, now that field day was over, Laura didn't mind leaving Ridgeview. And she probably wouldn't mind leaving Redfield either, other than having to suffer through another settling in with Mama.

3

RIGHT OFF THINGS WERE DIFFERENT in Redfield in that Mr. Turner didn't seem to mind Laura being around the place. Both Mr. Tuttle and Mr. Blair had made it clear she was to stay out of the barn, and they never looked too joyful to see her any other place either. But Mr. Turner had smiled and waved going by in his truck one afternoon as Laura was following Luther up the road to bring in the cows, and soon after, Daddy let her know just how welcome she was.

"I got something to discuss," he announced

as he came in from chores one evening. "Where's Ryan?"

Mama nodded toward the sound of the TV in the living room. "Where else? He's been fused to that thing since we came here. It's a shame, Dan. He was to pitch his first summer-league game tonight."

"I know, I know. I mind as much as you do, Franny." Daniel Cate scrubbed his fingers through his curly black hair. Sweat had streaked the dust on his tanned face, marking the lines around his eyes and mouth. His dark eyes now, though, were those of a child with a surprise. "Wait till you hear this. Laura, get Ryan in here and call Luther, will you? He's fiddling with the mower."

"Dad wants you," Laura yelled at the back of Ryan's red head on her way out the door to find Luther. He was sitting on the seat of the mower, looking over the fields and lake to where the setting sun was balancing on the highest peak of the mountains beyond.

"Look at that fireball," Luther said as Laura climbed up beside him. "Seems like those mountains would roar into flames when it touches them like that."

21

Laura squinched her hazel eyes to watch. "Their backsides burn," she said. "You'll see the glow in a little bit."

Luther looked at her with his smile that was mostly in his eyes. He was as dark as their dad but slighter. His straight hair fell over his eyes like an awning, so it could be a bit startling to catch him watching you in his intent way. "Tell you what else you can see," he said. "You watch along those woods, and pretty soon some deer will come out into the field. Been there every evening so far."

"Daddy wants to talk to us, and it's time to eat. Will they be there later?"

"We'll check it out." Luther jumped down, then turned his back to Laura. "Hop on, Laurie-bell. I'll give you a piggyback."

Laura hung on to Luther's neck, laughing as he staggered drunkenly through the grass and across the road.

"The two of you could raise the dead," Mama said from the screen door. "When's she going to be too big to haul around like that, Luther?"

"Never, far as I can see." Luther set Laura down on the steps. "The taller she gets, the skinnier. A breeze could land her in the lake."

"Well, get her in here where she can eat," Daddy ordered. "I got something to talk over."

Daniel Cate waited while his wife dished up the spaghetti. When he had something to say, he wanted full attention. "I been talking to Ralph Turner," he began when everyone was sitting down and looking at him, "and things are looking pretty good for us here."

He sensed a letdown, as Mama lowered her eyes and they turned to their eating. "Now, I mean it," he said. "I know I've made promises before, but this is different. The major thing is Turner's secure moneywise and he's got no interest in selling." Daddy scooped a huge swirl of spaghetti into his mouth, chewed, and washed it down with iced tea before continuing. "The man was born here and wants to die here, but he's been at it since he was Luther's age and before, and now he and the missus want some freedom to come and go. He'll keep a hand in, but they'd like to visit their daughter in Oregon, maybe try a couple months in Florida. So"—Daddy paused until all eyes were on him—"depending on how he finds me the next couple weeks, he'd like me to serve as farm manager.

He's raising me more than I'm used to, plus all the beef and milk we want."

Farm manager. That sounded good to Laura. They all looked at Mama, waiting for her reaction.

"Man could die tomorrow, Daniel," she finally said. "Then what?" Laura almost laughed. If that was the only flaw Mama could come up with, she must be impressed.

Daddy seemed to think so too, because he gave a little smile before answering.

"Life's got no guarantees, Franny, we all know that. But he's only fifty-eight and his father's still living over there with them close to ninety."

"Where's he going to stay when Turner and his wife take off for Florida?" Mama didn't look the least perturbed when Daddy shot her a look of pure irritation.

"I didn't ask, Franny, I don't see it as my place. Maybe Turner's got brothers or sisters who can take a turn. I'm sure they'll come up with something. Now can I get on with this?"

"Certainly, Daniel. I just like a clear picture." Mama wiped the corners of her mouth with her thumb and appeared ready to hear more.

"The thing is," Daddy continued, "I could

24

use a little help from Ryan and Laura here. They're old enough to be useful, and Turner's got no problems with them being around the barn. Now, how about it?"

At the mention of work, Ryan crossed his eyes and slid down in his seat as though he'd been clubbed. Laura, though, perked up. She liked helping Daddy and Luther with chores whenever they let her. Besides, the summer days were long, and she'd been running out of things to do.

Mama was folding and refolding her napkin. Even in the heat her plump, freckled arms looked cool and smooth as marble. "Two things, Daniel," she said. "You know how I feel about the boss paying one and working the whole family. Turner's already cashing in on Luther, not to mention myself helping out here and there. I don't want him freeloading off Ryan and Laura as well. Furthermore, with an opportunity like that, how come the last hand left so fast?"

"I'm only talking an hour, morning and evening, Franny, other than getting in the hay, and Turner said he'd pay the kids for helping there. Plus he's not taking a free ride on

Luther. He's giving him use of the truck and a little extra now and then. Not what he'd make on his own, I grant you, but right now what with this raise and all he's more valuable to us here, long as he's willing."

Laura could tell Daddy was going to ignore the second part of Mama's question, but Mama didn't let it go. "So why did the last hand leave so fast we were hired and here in two days?" she asked again.

Daddy took a swallow of iced tea. "I asked about that and I'm inclined to believe Turner, though it sounds peculiar and I don't want you to get all riled. Seems there's been a series of . . . of mishaps here. Odd things. House filling with smoke for no apparent reason, horrible smells that come and go, things missing or moved from one place to another. Nobody hurt, you understand, but I guess it near drove a couple wives crazy and they couldn't get out of here fast enough."

"So why shouldn't I get riled, Dan?" Mama sounded as if she already was. "Whoever heard of such goings on? What about that smell in our bedroom? If we got to live with stuff like that, I don't care how much Turner pays you."

"Take it easy, Franny. I'm going to check out that smell right this evening. I know it's not pleasant, but it's likely nothing fearful. Remember them baby coons got trapped in the chimney in Bakersfield? This smells roses in comparison."

"Kind of stuff you're suggesting's not as innocent as raccoons in the chimney and you know it, Daniel Cate."

"You're right, Franny, it isn't," Daddy agreed. "But Turner thinks he's figured it out and took steps to stop it. Seems some developer's got his eye on this land and was hoping to run Turner off. Turner put it right to him this last time and threatened to take action."

"Maybe Granger was in on it," Laura said. "Maybe he doesn't like sharing his house with anybody." She'd only seen Granger up close a few times, scuttling between the barn and his side door. He was a knobby little man with hunched shoulders. He wore his cap pulled down over thick glasses, and he stared at the ground as though his neck had stiffened in that one position.

"She could have a point, Daniel," Mama said. "He's right here to see the chances. I

27

spoke to him nice as can be and he didn't look at me once. Gave me pause, I'll tell you. Maybe he won't like it, you being made farm manager. Maybe he'll make trouble all on his own."

Daddy shook his head. "Granger's not looking for responsibility," he said. "He's a good enough worker, but he gets all shook if you get personal as a 'hello.' He may be peculiar, but I can't see him involved in something like those pranks."

"Maybe it's ghosts." Ryan spoke in a creaky whisper. He oogled his eyes at them in a rare show of interest. "Ghosts seeking revenge for a murder, a murder so vile the walls ooze with horror, the foundation shudders, the air sickens. . . ." Ryan's whisper had risen to a wail, and he was on his feet, clawing at his red hair and staring wildly about.

"Sit down, Ryan," Mama said calmly. "He should be an actor," she said to Daddy.

"Looks like he's taking his training in front of the TV." Daddy reached over and shook Ryan's shoulder. "So how about it? Can I count on you?"

"Do I have a choice?" Ryan was sullen again. "What if I have other plans?"

Daddy stopped smiling. "I think a boy near fourteen can share in what needs doing for his family. We got a chance here for a life that's a little more secure, and that benefits you as well as the rest of us. You got plans, and I ain't seen the evidence, we'll try to work with them. Other than that, I think you can manage a couple hours a day without too much damage. When I was your age, I was putting bread on the table."

"He'll help," Mama said. "It's just he's not partial to farm work like Luther."

"Now how's he to know?" Daddy asked. "He's never done it."

Daddy pushed back from the table. He'd had his say, one of the longest Laura could remember. She piled her dirty dishes on top of Ryan's. "Your turn to clean up," she said as she followed Luther outside to look for deer.

4

LAURA PUT HER HAND in her brother's as they walked down through the field to see the deer Luther said were sure to be there. She knew Mama worried about Luther spending so much time off by himself in the woods and fields. "It's a busman's holiday," she'd complained to Laura just that morning as they'd been laying new shelf paper. "He gets done caring for farm animals and he goes off looking for wild ones. Doesn't seem right, a boy his age." But as far as Laura was concerned, whatever Luther did was very much right. He had always been her special person in the family. It was Luther she'd told the time she'd been the only girl in the whole fourth grade not invited to Lisa Graves's birthday party. And she'd looked for him first to tell about winning the prize for the best Book Week poster. Luther even read to her sometimes from his Narnia books, while Mama had stopped as soon as Laura could read for herself.

They sat on a flat rock still warm from the sun. Luther pulled a stalk of timothy from its sheath and bit off the sweet end. His eyes were intent on the woods that bordered the field. The first star gradually brightened in the twilight sky, insects began to gossip, birds murmured an occasional good-night. "There, now," Luther said, soft as a breeze, as a doe and two fawns moved from the shelter of the trees. "There they are. You seen anything better than that?" The doe lifted her head and gazed directly at them. Then, keeping herself between them and her babies, she lowered her head to graze.

They watched until they could no longer distinguish the graceful shapes against the dark woods. "That mother and her twins have come every night since I been looking," Luther said as they walked back through the dew-damp field. "Sometimes others join them. I counted as many as eight one night, but always those three." He breathed in the night air as though it were water on a parched throat. "We tamper so in farming, it eases me to see what we leave be."

Laura could understand that. She always minded when the calves were taken from their mothers, and it was even worse when the bull calves were trucked away. "Luther," she began, intending to ask if he'd help her with a drawing of the twin fawns and their mother, when a slight movement up along the road caught her eye. She stopped and pulled on her brother's hand. "What's that? Over there, Luther, I saw something move over there." She wondered why her heart was pounding so, until she remembered what Daddy had said about weird things happening at this place. "Maybe it's that developer, come back to try to scare us off," she whispered, holding back as Luther continued toward the road.

"If someone's there, we'd better find out who," Luther said, peering in the direction Laura had pointed.

"What if he means trouble?" Laura still hung back, but Luther's calm "Come on, Laura, you sound like Ryan" was enough to get her moving. The shadow moved with them. "There," Laura said. "Somebody's over near that tree. Right across from the house."

"Probably Daddy or Granger," Luther said logically. "Maybe even old Ryan came out to enjoy the night."

Whoever it was moved slowly away from the tree, past the house, then stopped again before reaching the barn. "Hello there!" Luther's sudden call startled Laura into clutching at his arm. He dragged her along as he hurried toward the dark form. "Nice evening, eh?" he said as they got closer.

"They don't come no better'n this," an old man's voice wheezed from the darkness. "Can't hardly get my fill. Look at that now, you see the question mark up there? That's old Leo's head, and that triangle there, more to the east, that's his tail. Yep, old Leo's looking after the place tonight."

"Where, Luther?" Laura's fear was forgotten as she tried to find the pattern in the mass of glittering stars overhead.

"Over there, facing west." Luther tipped her head and pointed. And there it was, the curve of the back of the lion's head, the line of its reclining body, and the triangle tail.

"I *see* it." Laura's voice squeaked with the excitement of her discovery, and the old man laughed.

"He's there whether we see him or not, and to my mind there's no greater comfort than that. Time of year he's busy elsewhere, you got Orion or the old swan Cygnus watching out. You can see Cygnus coming along up there, ready to take over. Some people call it a cross, but it's a swan, sure enough, its wings spread wide."

But now Laura was more interested in making out who they were talking to. The old man was leaning heavily on a stick. From what she could see, he seemed to be wearing striped pajamas and a flat-brimmed hat.

"I'm Luther Cate, and this is my sister, Laura." Luther held out his hand, and the old man shifted his grip on the stick to take it.

"Pleased to make your acquaintance, I'm sure," he said. "Name's Turner, Isaac Turner. Took a fancy to visiting the old place. Margaret and I used to sit out on the porch there, nights like this, watching the deer, sniffing that honeysuckle till we was near drunk on it." His voice faded away and he was quiet, remembering. Then, "I best be getting back before Ralph and Noreen take notice. Farther than I reckoned. Set my mind on getting here; I forgot about the going back. Must be getting old. Folks been telling me so for years."

"I'll give you a lift," Luther said. "The truck's sitting right there by the barn."

"I'd be much obliged." The old man suddenly sounded very tired. "Don't know what I was thinking, coming out with just these slippers." Before she thought about it, Laura moved closer and took his free hand. They stood there hand in hand while Luther brought the truck around. Laura braced herself to support the old man as he climbed into the cab. She passed up his stick when he was settled on the seat next to Luther. "Thank you kindly," he said with grave courtesy. "Remember, little miss," he called when she slammed the door and they were about to drive off, "remember your friends up there." In the faint glow from the panel lights, Laura could see him motioning skyward with his stick.

"Where's Luther?" Mama asked when Laura came in alone.

"He's taking old Mr. Turner home in the truck." The closed windows and pulled shades of the living room were stifling. Daddy had already gone to bed. Ryan was slouched in his usual spot on the couch, rhythmically plopping his right fist into the pocket of his ball glove while he stared at a paper-towel ad on TV. Laura was used to Ryan saving his charm for everybody but them, but he'd never been this bad. She wanted to scream at him, shake him, anything to shatter his stupor. She settled for wrenching down the volume on the TV as she went by.

Ryan jerked bolt upright and shot his glove after her. "Whatcha doing, ya little creep? Turn it up." But Laura was already halfway up the stairs.

Mama followed and called from the bottom, "Mr. Turner? What's he doing up here?"

"Just enjoying the night," Laura called back. But Mama wasn't put off so easily. She puffed up the stairs and stood in the doorway of Laura's bedroom. "What do you mean, enjoying the night? Let him enjoy it at his own place. Aren't we entitled to a little privacy, for heaven's sake? Good thing I drew the shades. You watch out for him, Laura. Old men can get funny ideas."

"He wanted to smell the honeysuckle, Mama, and look at the stars."

"Oh," said Mama.

"And he got tired, so Luther took him home."

"That was right of Luther." Mama sighed. "I'm sorry, Laura. Each change we make, it takes me longer to get straight. Sometimes I just hate them all. The Tuttles and the Turners and the Blairs, all those owners who can toss us around simple as switching on a blender." Mama sank down on Laura's bed. "We'd hoped for a place of our own by now, but the way things are going, even those who have their own are losing them. I get to wondering if there's ever going to be a place for us, and your daddy not knowing or wanting anything else."

"It's almost the same, Daddy being farm manager, isn't it?" Laura had smoothed paper out on the floor and was looking for her colored pens.

"Nothing's the same as having your own

place, but it's sure a step up . . . if it works out. We've had promises before. Promises are part of poor people's wages. Your pens, if that's what you're looking for, are right over there." Mama nodded toward a packing box draped with Laura's pajamas. "I don't mind so much for your daddy and me. I might've chose a different life, more in one place and living in town, but I knew your daddy loved farming when I married him. Luther, now, though. What's he going to do? He should be training for something, but we can't spare him. And he ought to be out gallivanting with friends, instead of driving old Mr. Turner home."

Laura sighed. She hated it when Mama was full of sad talk. She made little yellow stars in a midnight-blue sky. "He's only sixteen, Mama. And he's nicer than any boy I've ever seen. Anybody would like him if they knew him."

"How's that going to happen with us moving hither and thither and yon and him working like he does? That's right pretty, Laura," she said of Laura's picture. "What are you arranging them like that for?"

"That's the constellation Leo," Laura said.

38

"Mr. Turner showed it to me." She decided to wait for Luther's help on drawing the deer. He was really good doing animals.

"Your Grampa Ryan knew the stars," Mama said unexpectedly. "When I saw our Ryan's red hair, I thought he was going to take after him, but Luther's more the one."

"Only stars Ryan ever looks at are holding baseball bats," Laura said sourly. She had one brother she adored, and then there was Ryan, interested in nothing but sports and TV and being cool for his friends. She didn't like to admit that being part of what he ignored could still hurt.

"Ryan's got dreams, Laura, and the stuff to back them up," Mama said tartly. "I got no worries about him wearing away on a farm. There are plenty of people willing to pay big money for talent like his." Mama seemed to take Laura's silence for a challenge. "Why, like the Ridgeview Recreation Department offering him a job this summer to coach the children's day-camp programs. They sought him out—he didn't even know the job existed. Getting paid to teach baseball and basketball and all those other games they play and he's not even out of junior high yet. Course it wasn't much and it's gone now, but it was an indication."

Grown-ups. Laura couldn't figure them out. Here was Mama all upset that Luther was on a dead-end road, while thinking Ryan had what counted. "Does that make sense to you, Riley?" she asked when Mama had gone and she was getting ready for bed. Of course it didn't.

5

ELLEN DAVIS, THE REGIONAL teacher for the Rural Education Program, came rattling down Valley Road one hot afternoon in her little tan Honda. Laura hadn't expected to see her again, but Ellen said she'd be visiting same as always since they were still in the same county. Redfield and Ridgeview felt like different worlds to Laura.

Mama greeted Ellen like a long-lost sister, and even Ryan got up from the TV when he heard her voice.

"Hey, Ryan," Ellen said when he drifted past her chair on his way to the refrigerator. "You coming to summer tutoring? Three mornings a week at the center, then I'll come by for some one-on-one. What do you say?"

"I'm not sure I'll do it," Ryan answered, avoiding Mama's eyes. "I got chores here, and I'm hoping to find a team."

"Redfield doesn't have one," Ellen said gently. "I already checked. The closest one is in Middlebury, and they've been picked and practicing over a month."

Ryan got some lemonade and went back to the TV without another word. Laura wished she could do something to make him feel better, but she couldn't think of a single action of hers that would matter much to Ryan. He had lost interest in her years ago.

"You don't need tutoring this year, Laura," Ellen was saying. "Your test scores are fine. I can bring you some reading enrichment stuff, though, if I work with Ryan."

"You'll work with him, no question about that," Mama said. "Daniel and I agree their education comes first. Course, we can't spare Luther, but he seems to be going along well enough. Ryan, though, I worry about him, Ellen." Mama drained the lemonade pitcher into Ellen's glass, then settled back in her chair. "He's resentful. It sticks out all over him like burdocks. He's a fish out of water right now, and I don't want to be on him when he's hurting, but Daniel's losing patience."

Laura drifted out to the porch. It was almost time to go for the cows. She and Ryan took turns bringing them in. This was the first week they'd gone alone without Luther. Laura was still a little nervous about what the cows might do when they saw she was by herself, but so far most of them had seemed ready to head for the barn at the end of the afternoon.

Laura hoped to get away on her bike before Mama noticed, but even with Ellen there Mama heard her going.

"You be careful now," she called from the door. "You hear me, Laura? Those cows aren't house pets."

Laura was down the road before her mother could say any more. She knew the cows weren't house pets. After all, she'd been there when Pete was carried out of Blair's barn with a broken pelvis. One of the cows had crushed him against a wall with a flip of her hindquarters, and Daddy said it hadn't been a troublesome cow either. But since she and Ryan had started chores, Mama had been dredging up stories of every accident and injury she'd ever heard of. When Daddy tried to calm her fears by saying those things usually happened handling the cows in close quarters, Mama took to ending her stories with ". . . and *that* happened right out there in the field."

Laura bumped along the cowpath to the far end of the pasture. Sheba, who considered herself queen, had seen Laura coming and was moving to take her place at the head of the procession. Laura already had her own names for some of the cows. Besides Sheba, there was old Cyclops, her one eye bulging from her head in a way that reminded Laura of the bobbly eyes on springs she'd seen in the Ben Franklin store. Sabrina was easily spooked, shying away from every passing bird or leaf, and Hyacinth, who wouldn't go near Ryan, sidled up to Laura with soft nuzzles.

True to form, Pisser developed a different plan the minute she saw the other cows moving toward the barn. Without lifting her head, she began grazing up toward the woods. "Come on, Pisser, come on," Laura called, and got off her bike to run after the stray. Pisser rolled her eyes at Laura and kept walking. Laura waved her arms and stamped. "Get along there, now," she ordered in as big a boss voice as she could manage.

Pisser wasn't fooled. She snorted and wheeled to charge past Laura back down the field. Laura leaped to one side, lost her balance, and fell directly on a bed of stinging nettles. The burning, itchy flame along the back of her bare leg sent her flying in a rage after the galloping beast.

"You get back here, you stupid Pisser!" she yelled, grabbing a stick for emphasis.

It could have been the brook that brought Pisser up short, but Laura preferred to think it was her own command. After all, the cow could easily have splashed across and continued along the other side. But there she stood when Laura puffed up, as agreeable as if they'd just shared a nice jog. She watched with interest as Laura sat down in the water to cool her burning leg, then followed as if attached to a string while Laura retrieved her bike.

Sheba was still leading the way up the field, but some of the herd had wandered off course. "Let's go! Let's go!" Laura shouted as she clattered back and forth on her bike. She followed them through the gate, past Luther's wink and Mr. Turner's smile, as though she'd been doing this all her life.

When she'd measured out the right number of scoops of grain for each cow and watered the calves, Laura went back across the road to help with supper. Mama wasn't in the kitchen, and the lemonade glasses from Ellen's visit were still on the table.

"Mama?" Laura called into the quiet of the house. "Mama?" She went into the living room, and there was Mama, sitting on the couch with the laundry spread all around her.

"It's starting again, Laura," she said in a flat voice. "We're barely calling this place home and they're starting on us."

"Who is, Mama? What's the matter?"

"You stop to take a look, you'll see soon enough. The buttons, Laura. There's not one button left, and no threads to show there were any. I only put a few things out this morning, other than the towels. Wouldn't take too much time to go through them, I guess, but some-body was out there snipping in broad daylight."

Sure enough, three shirts, a pajama top, and Laura's blue shorts lay flat and buttonless as paper-doll clothes at Mama's feet. Laura felt the urge to giggle, but instead she pulled her brow into a frown of concern. "Nothing was ruined, Mama," she said by way of comfort. "We can fix them."

"That's not the point, young lady, and you know it." Mama swept the clothes back into the laundry basket and carried it out to the kitchen.

When Daddy came in for supper, she word-lessly handed him one by one the debuttoned clothes. He stood holding them with a look of bewilderment on his face, while Mama turned back to the stove. "Take a look at that, Daniel, and tell me not to get riled," she said as she dished mashed potatoes into a bowl with vigorous plops.

"The buttons, Daddy," Laura murmured. "The buttons are gone."

"That's right." Mama jabbed at the carrots. "Every last one of them cut off those clothes as they hung on the line. I tell you, Daniel Cate, I

47

will not sew buttons every time I bring in a wash. Get that Turner to straighten this out, and now!"

Daddy caught Mr. Turner just as he was driving away from the barn. They went around back and stood toeing the grass under the clothesline as they considered the situation. Laura, peering from the kitchen window, could see them point up the road, then glance at Granger's back door. They shook their heads and clapped each other's backs as they parted.

"Well?" Mama stood with her hands on her hips as Daddy came in.

"Well, we're looking into it," Daddy said as he sat down at the table. "Turner's going up to town tomorrow, and we'll keep our eyes open around here. Says he hopes you're not the sort to turn tail and run."

"Fat chance and you know it, but don't let that rest you any easier." Mama took the meat loaf out of the oven and banged the door shut. "Now give a holler to those boys, Laura. It's time to eat."

CHAPTER

6

FOR A WHILE MAMA blamed every little puzzlement on the buttonsnipper. Her purse, which she insisted she'd left same as usual in the kitchen cupboard, was found in a little-used drawer. One of Daddy's barn boots seemingly walked itself across the road to hide under the porch steps, and Ryan's bike, if not tampered with, must have pedaled itself out of the shed to lie in the tall grass next to the pasture gate. But as one hot day simmered into the next, even Mama was lulled into accepting such everyday mysteries as just that.

The first chance she got, Laura rode up the road to investigate the brook she'd sat in the day she'd chased Pisser. It ran under the road through a big round culvert to continue along the far edge of the south field toward the lake. Laura leaned her bike against the post that marked the bridge for plows in the winter and slid down the side of the culvert.

The thickets of thorn bushes lining the brook on either side made Laura feel she was stepping into a secret tunnel. The sudden shade and the cold water sent a chill of goose bumps along her sweaty skin. Enclosed in its curtains, the water murmured to itself and stones shifted under Laura's feet with an echoey *thunk*. Bright fingers of sun reached between the leaves to probe the stream for treasures. Inching along, Laura pocketed a smooth, flat stone shaped like an L and a dark-red one dusted with gold glints. She found the best wishing rock she'd ever seen, a polished black stone circled with two bands of white crystal.

Bent double over the streambed as she was, it took Laura a while to notice that the brook had widened and slowed. She looked up to see that the tunnel opened to slender birch trees as the stream spread into the glistening horizon of lake beyond. Laura stood still. It was as if she were staring through the little window on one of those fancy Easter eggs, only instead of green grass with bunnies hiding among paintbox flowers, she was looking at blue, blue water sparked with diamonds and two little sailboats skimming along.

"Oh, Riley," she breathed, and splashed along to where the land folded back before the wide-open, sun-shimmered spaces of the water world. The lake lap-lapped at the shore, which was sandy beach for a stretch before it softened into the sucking mud of a marsh. Even the smell was different here, a sweetish smell richer than that of summer rain.

Laura waded out in her T-shirt and shorts until she was waist deep in the water. She wasn't supposed to swim alone. Mama said so often enough, but Mama was far away, and cooling off this close to shore wasn't really swimming. Laura was a good swimmer, more at home in the water than on land with what she could do with her body. She flipped into a back somersault, glided along the bottom, then sprang up through the surface and down again in what Luther called her dolphin dance. They'd gone swimming almost every day last summer in a pond just down the road from their trailer, but so far none of them had looked for a good spot here in Redfield.

Laura floated in close to shore and lay blowing bubbles on the surface of the water. A dragonfly hovered over her. A fish plopped farther out. Laura squinted her eyes almost shut against the glare until the brown sand, the green field that sloped up beyond it, and the blue sky shifted and swirled together like kaleidoscope patterns around a center pole. It was, Laura saw as she opened her eyes wider, a tree, a huge old tree standing alone in the field. It had four lower limbs spread level over the grass like some ancient compass. Even though not a leaf of its green bouquet stirred in the still air, Laura had the impression of massive arms reaching out to her.

She dripped out of the water and up through the tall grass. Those arms were easy to reach, as the tree provided a knee here and a hip there for steps. Laura climbed among the lower branches, then came down to sit in a hollow of the tangled roots with her back against the rough, warm bark. She felt as if she were on a throne, looking out on fields polka-dotted with flowers like Mama's sundress, at sailboats moving far out on the lake. She was vaguely aware, as she drifted off to sleep, of a most comforting feeling inside, as though a warm rain were melting little ice chips that had been frozen all through her.

Laura was late getting back for chores. Mama yelled at her because she'd been worried, and Daddy mumbled something about responsibility. Ryan could hardly get his own chores done, he was so busy smirking at her and rubbing "shame, shame" with his index fingers. Laura would have enjoyed jamming those fingers down his throat, but in spite of it all she was humming as she measured out the grain.

Luther smiled at her across the backs of the munching cows, and if he hadn't been so busy with the milking she probably would have told him then about the lake and the tree and the leafy tunnel. As it was, she told nobody, other than to say, when

Mama asked, that she'd been wading in the brook at the far end of the south field.

"You watch out for deep spots," Mama warned. "You know how I feel about playing around water."

Laura nodded. "The brook is shallow," she said, keeping her fingers crossed to cover her swim in the lake.

After supper she went upstairs and spread a long strip of newsprint on her bedroom floor. She drew a lacy green tunnel with slender birch trees clustered at the end. She drew a streambed, with a silver line for the water and bright-colored pebbles scattered like jewels in a jumble of brown and mossy-green rocks. Then she drew the lake, one view framed by birch trees, another showing the beach and the marsh grass. Finally Laura drew the tree, with its arms reaching wide over the flowered field.

She sat for a long time, studying the pictures spread across the floor. Then in tiny letters because it was her secret, she wrote *The Godmother Tree* under the last picture. After more thought, she printed *Loria* under the view of the lake framed by the birch trees at the end of

the tunnel. Loria, she decided, because it reminded her of the mystical world of Narnia in
Luther's C. S. Lewis books, and Loria because
it was hers.

CHAPTER

7

LAURA SPLASHED DOWN the brook to Loria every chance she got, but Mama didn't make it easy to get away. After Ryan started his tutoring, she seemed worried Laura would feel left out. "Come help me with the garden," she would say, although at first that had been her own private celebration of a sure summer in one place. She insisted Laura go with her when she went to Redfield for groceries, then pointed out every single kid who looked anywhere near Laura's age. "That girl over by the orange juice is looking your way, Laura. The least you could

56

do is smile." Laura politely refrained from reminding Mama she hadn't made the least effort
toward Mrs. Turner, the only woman living
within two miles of them. "I won't have
Noreen Turner sticking her nose up at me,"
Mama had said the one time Daddy asked her
to take something over.

Even Mama, however, ran out of things for
Laura to do. One particularly hot morning
Laura pedaled for the brook as though flames
were licking at her back. A fly droned around
and around her head as she sped along, and her
mosquito bites itched beyond endurance. She
dropped her bike in the grass, slid down the
side of the culvert, and fell full-length into the
cool water.

"Another hot one, that's the truth." Laura
jerked upright at the sound of the dusty voice.
A wheezing laugh drew her attention to the
culvert. "Startled you, eh? Well you gave me a
bit of a turn yourself."

Old Mr. Turner was sitting on a rock with
his feet in the brook just inside the shadow of
the culvert. His white shins gleamed below
black trousers rolled to the knee. As Laura's
eyes adjusted, she saw he had on his flat-

brimmed straw hat and a long-sleeved white shirt striped with suspenders.

"Better watch your step there, little miss. You could take a nasty spill. Almost did myself, getting down here." He nodded toward skid marks on the steep bank, then winked at her. "No other place to be on a day like this. 'Hottest stretch of weather I can remember,' Noreen says this morning. 'Like as not it's some kind of record,' but I tell her I can remember hotter. Why, back 1911 it got up to one hundred and six in the shade on the Fourth of July. Only celebration we could muster was a thank-you-Lord our blood didn't boil right out of us. But for overall hot, I'd say summer of twenty-one gets the prize."

The old man was looking somewhere past Laura. He smiled and shook his head. "I was courting Margaret that summer and having second thoughts," he went on. "She never could take the heat, turned her crotchety as an old hen. Married her anyway . . . figured I was safe long as we stayed in Vermont. Yep, lived here all my life, right up there at the farm till Ralph and Noreen took it in their heads they wanted a fancier place. Built a one-story thing and painted it blue, can you fathom that? Sky's blue, houses are white, I say."

Isaac Turner's voice trailed away as he sat staring down at his own pictures in the water. Laura waited awhile, then said softly, "It was nice seeing you again."

The old man jerked his head up as she turned away. "Eh? What's that? You going along now? I'd go with you if I could. Give anything for another look at that old tree. Margaret and I used to take a picnic . . ." He gazed after her, but Laura could tell, glancing back, that he was seeing someone else.

Loria looked different every time she approached. This morning the still lake gleamed rather than glinted, as though ironed flat by the heavy heat. Laura swam back and forth along her beach, careful to stay in shallow water so she wouldn't feel guilty about going against Mama. She gazed up at the godmother tree, spreading shade over the baking field. She remembered Daddy saying old Mr. Turner was close to ninety, and he had come to the tree. It must have been there way back in olden times. Laura imagined ladies with big hats and long skirts coming to sit by the lake in its shade;

little children in knickers and gingham dresses climbed through its branches. Long gingham dresses and high-top shoes like she'd seen in Gramma Ryan's picture album.

Laura started toward the tree, wringing the edges of her shorts and T-shirt as she went. Her hair was dripping over her face. She shook it back, but the dark and light spaces of her view through it didn't clear and she realized she was looking at a cow, a black-and-white cow grazing in the shade of the tree.

Laura walked slowly closer. The cow lifted her head, then went back to eating. "Hello there," Laura said. She bet this was the cow Daddy had been worrying over. She was about to give birth and had wandered away from the north pasture, where he'd been keeping an eye on her. He'd never think to look here.

"You look like you had your baby," Laura observed. "Where is it?"

The cow looked back over her shoulder, away from the lake. "Up there?" Laura moved carefully to the right and began to circle toward a wild rose thicket behind the tree. The cow rolled wary brown eyes at her and moved along from the other side. They reached the thicket at the same time and stood at opposite ends, watching each other.

"It's in there, isn't it?" Laura tried to make her voice as gentle as the little breeze that stirred over them like a breath from the old tree. The cow stood quietly as Laura worked her way around the wild roses, parting the prickly branches to peer inside.

Just as she was deciding that it was impossible for anything to be crammed into that thorny tangle, she saw it, a softly gleaming black calf looking back at her with brown pansy eyes. "Ah," Laura breathed as the calf struggled to its feet and moved out to nuzzle its mother. "She's perfect, absolutely perfect."

The baby had a white diamond in the middle of its forehead and four matching white socks. Other than that, it was polished black. Laura reached her hand slowly toward the calf to test the mother's reaction. The cow skidded her eyes around but otherwise made no protest. As Laura stood stroking the warm, silky fur, trying to decide what to do, the cow gave an impatient snort and moved a few yards away. She looked back, and the calf followed. The decision was made: They were heading back.

It was slow going. The calf, Laura discovered, seemed to walk better backward. The mother would go a few yards, the baby would back after her, while Laura followed with a steady stream of encouragement. Every now and then the cow looked imploringly at Laura as though having second thoughts, but Laura held firm. "Keep going," she'd say, shooing her along with a sweep of the arm, and the cow obliged, sometimes ambling straight ahead, sometimes stopping to graze and consider the view.

"This could take all day, Riley," Laura sighed when they finally reached the high point in the field. The heat shimmered over the fields like a layer of gelatin. She watched a car trail a chute of dust along the road as the cow munched the sweet grass and the calf dreamily drank milk at her side. Laura waved, then turned back to urge the pair on after their snack. The next time she looked up, Luther was coming toward them.

All Laura could manage was a huge grin. Her relief at seeing her brother showed just how worried she'd been, afraid that the baby couldn't handle the trip, or that she shouldn't have tried to bring them back alone.

"She's a beauty," Luther said, rewarding Laura with his intense, approving look before he bent to caress the silky coat. "Dad will be pleased as all get-out. Mr. Turner was moaning about this old girl all morning."

"How did you know where we were?" Laura asked.

"We were up along the road mending a break in the north fence when some guy came along and said he'd seen you waving. Here now, you reassure Mama-girl and I'll give baby a ride." Luther knelt beside the calf and shouldered her as easily as a scarf. He shrugged her into a more comfortable position and started off, the cow trotting along behind now and Laura describing how she'd found the calf and got it to come as far as she had. Neither Luther then nor Daddy later asked how she happened to be way down in that field. They seemed to think she'd just wandered in a lucky direction that day.

Luther had parked the truck by the culvert. They loaded Laura's bike and rode back to the barn at a walking pace. Laura sat in the back with the calf stretched across her legs, while the mother, tied to the tailgate, sauntered along behind.

The calf was napping on a bed of fresh hay when Daddy and Ralph Turner came in. They joined Laura at the side of the pen to look it over. "Nice a one as we've had this year," Mr. Turner judged. "You done a fine job, Elsbeth," he said to the mother, who was peering over the slats across from them, "though I wish you could see your way clear to doing it a bit closer to home."

Daddy laid his heavy arm across Laura's shoulders. "I'm right proud of you, girl," he said, and that was enough.

CHAPTER

8

"Elsbeth and I think it only proper you name the calf," Mr. Turner said next morning to Laura at chores. "Anything you come up with is fine, anything at all."

"Rose," Laura said promptly. "Her name is Rose."

"Kinda nice having young'uns around," she heard Mr. Turner tell Daddy a few minutes later. "My own never took to farming. Couldn't get them near the barn to save my soul after they were of an age to be any help."

After that, Laura spent almost as much time

in the barn as she did at Loria. When she wasn't visiting Rose, she built a maze with hay bales up in the loft. She dragged some bales to the big open door and made a couch where she could read or draw. Laura didn't even try to keep out of Granger's way anymore. She'd noticed he was gentle with the cows, and the day she found the ginger cat's four kittens tucked away in a corner of the grain room, she was so excited she grabbed the only person around, who happened to be Granger, to come and see.

"Aw, l-l-lookee there, l-l-lookee there," Granger crooned in a voice harsh with disuse. "Sh-sh-she's a good mother, she is." Laura was completely won over and threatened to tell Daddy the next time Ryan made head-tapping, finger-twirling signs behind Granger's back.

Ryan blamed Granger when someone messed with the garden, and Mama was open to agreeing with him. Although she'd been late planting seeds and setting out the tomato and pepper plants Uncle Ed had given her, Mama had lavished such care on the garden, it had leaped up in response. Daddy joked that if he got half the attention her precious plants did, he'd think he'd died and gone to heaven.

Laura was still washing the breakfast dishes the morning Mama rushed in with tears streaming down her cheeks to say someone had been at her garden. "I expected woodchucks, maybe even deer, but not this, Laura, not this."

Laura ran out to see what had happened and stood looking around at the tomatoes in their wire cages, the peppers on a raft of black plastic, and the green rows headed by bright flags of seed packets on sticks. "What's the matter, Mama? It looks fine to me."

"Somebody's tampered with it." Mama sniffed. "After all the work I did planning and planting and caring for it, somebody's gone and tampered. It's plain meanness, that's what it is, just plain meanness." She blew her nose on a tissue from her sundress pocket.

Laura still couldn't see the trouble.

"Look there," Mama said, pointing. "And there. And over by the edge. Somebody's switched a good half of my pepper and tomato plants, and they moved my cherry tomatoes from the sunny corner to way up back in the shade. It's senseless—why would anyone?"

When Mama pointed it out, Laura could see that some of the plants in the wire cages were peppers and some spiking through the black plastic were tomatoes. The ones out of place were droopy from their move; in the corner where the cherry tomatoes had been, a dead bird lay feet up on the smoothed-over earth.

"No real harm's been done, Franny," Daddy said after he'd disposed of the bird at lunchtime. "I'm as flummoxed as you are about this, but the plants haven't been ruined. They'll grow where they are, or you can get Ryan or Laura to help you move them back."

"What about the bird, Daniel? Don't you see that as more than a cute prank?" Mama stood with her hands on her hips, glaring at Daddy as though he'd had a hand in the whole scheme.

"I don't know, Franny." Daddy rubbed a hand over his face. "Turner thought he'd dealt with the other trouble, and I'm inclined to agree. Once something like that's out in the light, it don't make sense to carry it on. That developer guy looked purely astonished when Turner put the laundry situation to him. He threatened to take action for false accusation. Not that he would, with what Turner's got on him previous, but it don't seem likely he's involved now."

"Then how do you explain this?" Mama demanded. "Turner may think he can handle the situation, but lakefront property like he's got might justify any lengths to a wrong sort. My garden's nothing compared to the safety of my kids. Am I going to have to worry every time they go off? Look at Laura here, running around exploring the place, and Ryan off on his bike. Can Turner guarantee their safety?"

"Don't worry yourself into a stew, Franny. We're not dealing with the Mafia here. We'll get to the bottom of it, I promise you that. Now come on, can't we have some lunch?" Daddy raised his hand to pat Mama's shoulder, but she brushed it off.

"I can't make light of this, Daniel. Somebody was here and messed with my garden, just like somebody messed with my laundry. And that bird was to scare me, lying feet up like that."

"It's got to be Granger." Ryan had come around the house and was examining the scene like some TV detective. "He probably had more blackbirds than he needed for his pie, so he left one for you when he rearranged your garden."

"Why would Granger do a thing like that?" Mama asked. "You see anything, Ryan, you better speak up."

"I didn't *see* anything," Ryan said, "but everybody knows Granger's nuts. He could be working for somebody. Living right here, this stuff would be easy."

"He's got a point, Daniel," Mama said. "Who else can tell the coast is clear?"

"That's the trouble—something like this, you start suspecting your own. Granger's been nothing but helpful to me. I seen you mocking him, Ryan, and I don't like it. I don't like your bad-mouthing him, neither." Daddy turned on his heel and headed for the house.

"What's he blaming me for? I was only trying to help." Ryan gave his bike a vicious kick before clattering around the house and off in the direction of the town road. Mama shook her head and sighed.

"The garden's bad enough without you coming down on Ryan." Mama's voice drifted through the kitchen window a moment later.

Laura stood looking at the drooping plants. The dead bird made the whole thing more sinister. There was something tickling the back of her mind, but she couldn't get it to focus. She took her sandwich up to her room and sat in the chair by the window to think. Her room was a nice place to be now. Uncle Ed had brought a real bed, the chair, and a bureau from Gramma Ryan's attic, and Luther had helped her make shelves from boards and crates for her books and games. Her drawings were tacked over the worst places on the walls, and Mama said if she saw a decent buy on a rug, she'd get it.

Laura looked out across the field and went back in her mind over what had happened. Mama had come in crying about the garden. Laura had gone out to look at it. She was going to get the shovel and throw the bird up back in the brambles, but Mama had said no, leave it so Daddy could see when he came in. Daddy had taken the bird first thing to the pit where they buried their garbage. Ryan had been gone all morning mowing Turner's lawn. . . .

Suddenly the tickle snapped into place. Ryan hadn't seen the garden until after Daddy threw the bird away, yet he seemed to know it was a blackbird and right where it had been.

Instead of swooshing down to her stomach, Laura's tuna fish sandwich was sticking along the way. Either Ryan had seen somebody put that bird in Mama's garden or he'd done it himself. And it couldn't have been Granger, or Ryan would have said so for sure, rather than just suggesting it.

Laura reached for her blanket and wound her fingers back and forth through the soft fringe of the frayed corner. Even though Ryan was not her favorite person, she didn't want to think he would do that to Mama's garden. She knew Ryan was ashamed of them. He hadn't let Mama fetch him at school since fifth grade, and he'd told his stuck-up friends at Ridgeview that Daddy worked for IBM. But this was different. This was very different.

She wasn't going to think about it. Daddy had said that was the danger of something like this, suspecting your own. For Ryan to hurt Mama, who went overboard to see his side of things, would be as crazy as him wrecking his precious ball glove.

Even after visiting Rose, Laura's thoughts still crowded her like a persistent horsefly. She got her bike and headed for Loria. She was scared, she realized when she was sitting up on her favorite branch in the godmother tree: scared that something was really wrong with Ryan, something that would make it possible for him to do a thing like this. And she was scared about what all this might do to Mama, who even in her worst times always came around to believing that life was going in a good direction, with the help of her nudges and be-carefuls.

Laura breathed in the sweetish smell of the lake, of sunbaked grass and green leaves. Gradually, the jagged edges inside her smoothed and fit back into place. She would talk to Luther when he got back from trucking heifers to Salisbury, but otherwise she'd just let things be for now. After all, Ryan *had* sat with her on the bus that awful first day in Redfield, and once he'd bought her a Fudgesicle when she'd gone to one of his games. Kids at school, especially girls, always liked Ryan right off. Laura had understood why when she watched him play ball; then his eyes and his mouth cleared and he looked real nice.

As she sat there breathing with the summer song of insects, Laura could think of some perfectly reasonable explanations for what Ryan had done and said.

9

As it turned out, Laura didn't talk to Luther about Mama's garden, because by the time she got back with the cows, Luther was gone again and the garden forgotten. Daddy was silent and stony faced at milking, and Mr. Turner, picking up Luther's share, was too busy for even a smile. Granger went about muttering and shaking his head, and Ryan's eyes, for once, were more serious than sullen.

"What happened?" Laura whispered to him in the grain room. "Where's Luther?"

"He's gone off," Ryan said without lifting his

head from his sweeping. "He's feeling bad."

"Why?" Laura asked. For a minute she thought Ryan, who loved to be first to tell bad news, was not going to answer.

He finally stopped sweeping and glanced at her before looking away. "Because," he said, and paused. "Because he hurt some deer. He was finishing that slope near the woods with a sickle bar and he mowed the legs off two little fawns lying in the grass. He came up and got the rifle to finish them off, then he took off in the truck. Dad went down and found them. I had to help dig a hole at the edge of the field to bury them so we'd be back when you brought the cows in." Ryan's voice had no more expression than if he'd been reading aloud from a geography book. He wiped his nose with the back of his hand and continued his sweeping.

Laura did her chores like a machine going through its cycles. She measured the right number of scoops of grain for each cow, she brought water for Rose and the other calves, she hayed the heifers. She even hosed the floor around the bulk tank that held the milk before removing her barn boots and crossing the road to the house. Mama was at the sink scrubbing potatoes. She looked up when Laura came in. "You heard?"

Laura nodded. She set four places at the table, carefully lining the silverware with the knife blades curving toward the plates. She folded paper napkins into triangles and put one under each fork. Then, when Mama was done at the sink, she collected mixing bowls and spoons, cake tins and rack, plus an assortment of drinking glasses, and filled the sink for washing, leaving enough space for rinse water. When the cooking dishes were draining, she wiped the counter clear back around each of the pine canisters that had been Mama's prize find at a garage sale down the road from Blairs' last year.

"The boy's too sensitive," Mama said as she stirred up a pitcher of iced tea. "Always has been, ever since he could take notice. Used to cry over every dead bird and animal in the road so's I'd hate to drive out shopping for fear of what he'd see. 'Things live, things die, and you'd better get used to it,' I'd say to him. 'You'll wear yourself out, taking it so to heart, 'specially on a farm.'"

"It's the machines," Laura said. "Cars, and

the mower, and guns. He feels animals don't have a fair chance. That's what bothers him. Not a natural dying but people's machines." She wrung out the dishrag and draped it neatly over the faucet. "Is there anything else you need me for?" she asked.

Mama looked up in surprise. "Not until the stew's done. Thank you, Laura, you've been a real help. Now where are you going?" she asked as Laura started out the door. "Don't you go off mooning over this. It's been a day I'd like to forget, but that's no reason not to eat. You need your strength to handle these things."

"Don't worry, Mama, I'll be right out back." Laura went around the end of the house to a tangle of bushes and vines and flowers at the edge of where they mowed. She'd found all kinds of flowers in that jungle, as well as raspberries, blackberries, and some other berries she'd been afraid to try. Mama said it was someone's old garden, and she knew the names of the stuff, too. Lupin, day lilies, sweet William, delphinium. Laura tried to remember the names as the flowers came and went. She picked delphinium and daisies now, mallow, and some little purple bells on a stalk, then fringed the bouquet with Queen Anne's lace.

Mama watched as Laura filled a canning jar with water and tried to fit the flowers in. "You need something bigger," she said, and found a gallon jug in the pantry that was just right. She seemed to know without asking what Laura intended. "That's most thoughtful of you, honey," she said as Laura carried the bouquet out of the kitchen.

Luther had done more for Laura's room than he had for his own. Other than his mattress, all he had were two sofa cushions propped on the floor, a crate holding his notebook, his set of Narnia books, pieces of wood he had collected, and a tall, narrow bureau whose top was littered with things from his pockets. Laura put the flowers on top of the crate. That was all she could do, for now anyway.

Luther was not one to let them lie awake with anxiety. He came back around nine, apologized quietly for missing chores, and went up to his room. Daddy followed him to the bottom of the stairs, then sighed and went into the bathroom to wash up for bed.

Luther was back at work the next day same as usual, though Laura noticed Daddy finished mowing the slopes by the woods. Mama said bad things happened in threes, and this time she was right, because less than a week later Mr. Turner came to the house first thing in the morning to say his father had died in the night. Laura felt the way she used to when a tooth came out, leaving an emptiness whose edges shivered when air touched them. She'd only seen the old man twice, but he'd been ready to visit, and he liked stars and honeysuckle and the godmother tree.

She was glad he hadn't been sick. "Not a day in his life," Mr. Turner said. "He just didn't wake up this morning, and that's all I asked for him." The Turners were leaving soon for Oregon, and in a way the old man's death made it easier for them to go.

"Now didn't that work out pretty," Mama said when Mr. Turner had gone. She was never very charitable when it came to bosses' families, but she sent Ryan over with some blueberry muffins. "Bread's the best thing in hard times," she told Laura. "It has a settling effect."

Bread didn't seem to help Luther any. He did what was expected of him, but his face was like a closed door with a No Trespassing sign on it. Laura missed him even when he was sitting right across from her at the supper table, for she couldn't see into Luther's dark room and he didn't look out. Mama, who attacked problems relentlessly in the belief she had the full range of solutions and just had to find the right one, seemed to know she could do nothing for Luther this time. To Laura's surprise, she even agreed to go up to Alburg with Uncle Ed to visit Gramma Ryan.

"I've begged and pleaded for her to come here," Mama said when Uncle Ed came by with the invitation, "but she says she gets a ringing in her ears if she drives more than a few miles, or her arthritis is acting up, or her cat frets if she so much as goes to get her hair done. Daniel was right when I was knocking myself silly to fix a place for her to stay here. Ma wouldn't leave that house of hers if we invited her to Buckingham Palace."

"Don't take it personal, Franny," Uncle Ed soothed. "Ma came to our place just once, in seventy-eight, when her furnace went on the blink and belched smoke all over the house. Barbara's stopped going up with me for the most part . . . says if Ma wants to be a hermit, who's to interfere?"

"She wants us there, you know that as well as I do, Ed. If that's the only way I get to see her, Laura and I will ride along with you this weekend. I'll bring a cake for her eightieth birthday. I'd hoped to have a celebration for her here, but if she won't budge out of that house, she'll have to take her celebration when she can get it."

Laura was as ready as Mama to leave Redfield behind for a couple of days, but she felt bad leaving Luther the way he was. She had been going to offer him Loria, the only healing she knew, but Luther had shut himself away so, there had been no openings.

The night before they left, Laura went across to the hayloft. She sat in the open door, looking over the twilight fields to the smoky lavender remains of a fiery sunset. In the fading light she spread some paper on the old cookie sheet she used for a drawing board, then carefully drew a map, starting at the culvert, of the leafy path to Loria.

When she went upstairs that night, Luther's door was open and his room dark. She tiptoed in and put the map under the edge of the flower jug. She fell asleep eased. Luther would see the birch gates opening to the lake, and he would probably find the beach, but just in case he was still all in himself and not noticing much, she had labeled the godmother tree and further marked it with a big star.

·

CHAPTER

10

LAURA LIKED UNCLE ED. He and Aunt Barbara ran a feed store over near Middlebury. The Cates didn't see much of Aunt Barbara, but Uncle Ed came by when he could. He was a big man, with blue eyes like Mama and Ryan and curly, sandy hair. Laura had noticed people started smiling when Uncle Ed appeared; the way he talked and laughed tended to air out a place.

Uncle Ed and Aunt Barbara didn't have any children. Mama figured one reason Aunt Barbara didn't come often was it bothered her to see how much Ed liked being around his niece and nephews. Ed was the one who had given Luther his Narnia books, and he and Ryan were always trying to stump each other on baseball trivia. He taught Laura such things as the difference between knots, hitches, and splices, but best of all were the stories he told about Great-Aunt Alice.

Aunt Alice was a doctor who traveled the remote areas of South America, living awhile here and awhile there to share what she could of her medical skills. Every three or four years she came back to visit Gramma Ryan in the house they'd both been born in, but she stayed only briefly and sometimes even Mama didn't get to see her.

"She has far more interest in total strangers than she does her own family," Mama grumbled. "She'd still be right here with the rest of us if she hadn't married a rich man who died and left her bundles of money."

But Uncle Ed told stories of canoe trips along the Amazon and of treks to mountain villages high up in the Andes, setting broken bones and delivering babies as she went. Laura learned more listening to Uncle Ed's stories about

Aunt Alice's travels than she did in any geography lesson at school. Better than that, though, was the sense of adventure the stories stirred in her, as if Aunt Alice's experiences might in some way be hereditary.

Gramma must have been watching for them, for as soon as they turned into her drive, she opened the front door and came out onto the steps to greet them.

"You must all be exhausted," she said, as though they'd just driven straight through from Florida instead of the two hours from Redfield. "Where's Ryan?"

"Hello, Ma." Laura's mother dropped the load she was carrying to hug Gramma. "Ryan doesn't like to travel any more than you do, and besides, it would have been hard for Daniel to spare him as well as Laura right now."

After Gramma had hugged and exclaimed over her, Laura went first thing to the pantry between the dining room and kitchen to measure herself against the marks that were dated and labeled with either an E or F. She was very pleased to see that she was a good three inches taller than her mother had been at the same age.

"Guess you're going to be tall and skinny like the Cates," Gramma said when Laura reported the results, "though Alice was the tallest girl in her class right through sixth grade; then people shot on past her and she didn't grow another inch. Left her feeling powerful about herself even so, while I always was a runt and knew it."

"Now that's just not true, Ma," Laura's mother said. "Keeping this house single-handed . . . and that garden. I don't know how you do it, with your knees."

"It's the best this year it's ever been," Gramma acknowleged. "I already put up more beans and pickles than I'll ever use. You remember to take some back, you two, and did you see my dahlias? They were in the Sunday paper with a color photo and all, though it didn't begin to do them justice. People come by this way just to look at them."

"You've always created beauty, Ma. There's no greater gift. Isn't that right, Ed?"

Ed was leafing through the stack of Aunt Alice's letters that Gramma had kept for them to read. "No argument there," he said. "I planted those bulbs you gave me, Ma, and the results are downright pathetic. Missed your touch, no two ways about it."

"You two stop it, now. You're just trying to make an old lady feel good." Gramma's eyes were bright as she tugged the corners of her mouth back into line. "Come on, Laura, let's see what we can find for lunch. You flatterers can walk up to say hello to the Holdens at the store and bring back some chocolate ice cream to go with that cake you brought."

After lunch—which had been more like a feast, with baked ham and scalloped potatoes and all the pickles and jellies and breads Gramma always put out—Laura went through the gap in the hedge to knock at the Lelands' back door. The Lelands had lived next door to Gramma since before Laura was born. Their only child was closer to Ryan's age, but Mary Sue Leland and Laura had played together whenever Laura visited Alburg since they'd been old enough to cross through the hedge to each other's yards.

They always played the same thing, a game they invented called Around the World. Each episode involved a rescue mission in some far-off place, a job so dangerous only they had the skills and courage to try it. The trick was to think up a mission for each game that would earn them the undying gratitude of the people they helped. Mary Sue was mainly interested in plots that had her save handsome young men, who then fell in love with her. Laura thought up such details as training eagles to airlift precious medical supplies and riding rhinoceroses down rivers full of hungry crocodiles.

"Why, Laura Cate, what a surprise! Goodness, how you've shot up!" Mrs. Leland held the screen door wide. "Mary Sue's in her room, dear. Just go on up. Your gramma didn't drop a word about this visit, though I haven't seen her to talk to in a few days."

Mary Sue was coming down the stairs as Laura reached the hall. At least that's who Laura assumed it was when she saw the tanned, bikini-clad girl with the perfect wedge haircut. "Laura!" Mary Sue squealed. "Oh my God, I can't believe it!" She rushed down the last few steps to lay her cheek briefly against Laura's and overwhelm her with hair-spray fumes. "What am I going to do?" she implored breathlessly. "I'm meeting Sam and Jeannie . . .

Wait a minute! Get your bathing suit and come with us. It'll be a blast. . . ." Even Mary Sue looked doubtful about that.

"Thanks, Mary Sue. I just came over to say hi. We're going back tomorrow, so I should stay with Gramma." Laura retreated as fast as she could, burning with embarrassment that she had thought Mary Sue might be interested in her latest idea for Around the World.

Gramma was resting on a lawn chair in the yard when Laura came back through the hedge. "She's changed, hasn't she?" she responded to Laura's silence. "Two years make a lot of difference at that age." Laura was absolutely certain she would never look like that in two years, not even with the help of a beauty-parlor hairstyle or a bikini tan. She longed for the godmother tree, where she could cry out the ache in her throat, the awful feeling of rejection and betrayal. She felt like she had when they'd moved to Tuttles' and the girl sitting nearest her in school returned her smile with a loud "She stinks!" Laura had never forgotten the shock and the sickening sense of shame over she hadn't known what. She'd been wearing a brand-new dress Uncle Ed and Aunt

Barbara had given her for her birthday, and Mama made her take a bath every school night.

When she'd sobbed the story out to Mama later, Mama traced the smell to Laura's red cardigan, which had been hanging on the hook next to Daddy's barn jacket. Laura had never worn the sweater again, even though Mama washed it with perfumed fabric softener and said Laura was foolish to let a rude little girl like that get the best of her. But Mary Sue Leland hadn't been rude. The one friend Laura could always come back to just wasn't there anymore.

"Bring that chair over and sit with me, Laura," Gramma said quietly. With a start, Laura realized that Gramma had been watching her from behind her sunglasses. Neither spoke for a long while, and Laura was beginning to think Gramma had dropped off to sleep when she started to talk. "I've lived in this house, in this town, my entire life, Laura, but I've never felt at home the way Alice does gallivanting all over the world. It's inside, that at-homeness. It's being your own best friend. I'm beginning to see I haven't been a very good friend to myself, Laura. Don't you make the same mistake. Don't nurse the hurts into monsters."

"I won't," Laura promised politely, although she didn't have much of an idea what Gramma was talking about. She watched a squirrel swing from branch to branch in the ash tree over their heads, then said without planning to, "Come and visit us, Gramma. You'll like the view."

Gramma got up, straightened her cotton dress, and tucked back her white hair. "I just might do that, young lady," she said. "Now how about calling your mama and your uncle Ed for some lemonade and ginger cookies."

C H A P T E R

11

NOTHING FELT RIGHT when Laura and Mama got back from visiting Gramma. Mama's garden was all droopy from lack of rain, and the flies, which defied all their efforts to eliminate them, frazzled the indoor air like electric currents. Another edge of wallpaper had come loose in the kitchen, and Mama found a dead rat on the cellar floor when she went down to change a fuse.

"You figure how to keep your flies and rats in the barn, Daniel Cate, or I'm taking the kids to Alburg," Mama hollered at Daddy, who turned around and went back to the tractor without taking so much as a bite of his lunch.

Luther seemed better. His eyes were back to noticing, but he stayed in his room with the door shut most of the time when he wasn't working. Ryan, now that summer tutoring was over, hardly ever left the TV. The noise of it always in the background was as irritating to Laura as the flies. Rose had developed scours, a highly contagious intestinal upset, and while Daddy didn't think it was a bad case, he didn't want Laura playing with her for fear of spreading it to the other calves.

Old Cyclops's bulgy eye got so bad Daddy had to put her down. "She was near the end of her production anyway," he told Laura, as if that would make her feel better about it. With Cyclops gone and Rose sick, Laura became more businesslike about her chores. She often finished ahead of Ryan, and that was how she found the glove.

Ryan had ridden his bike to town one morning to get some canning-jar lids for Mama. When Laura came up from the barn ahead of him that evening, Mama was ladling zucchini relish into a row of pint jars.

"Where'd that boy put those jar lids?" she asked Laura. "I got to get them on here while the stuff's still hot."

"I don't know," Laura said, glancing around at all the obvious places. "Want me to go ask?"

"I don't have time for that. Check his jacket pockets, will you?"

Laura looked on the sofa, then in Ryan's room. His jacket wasn't on the bed, so she went to the closet. Two shirts and a pair of school pants were hanging along the rod. Laura stuck her head in to check the hook partway down the wall, and there was Ryan's ball glove, slashed strips dangling limply from the strap. Laura could tell that Ryan had worked hard to shred the heavy leather like that. She knew he had done it. Who else would have? And she knew just as certainly that it had been Ryan who had messed up Mama's garden.

Laura felt as if her own stuffing had been ripped out of her. "Oh Riley, what should I do?" She stood uncertainly in the doorway of the closet. Then with sudden decision, she took the ruined glove back to the kitchen.

"Did you find the lids?" Mama was scraping the last of the relish from the kettle.

"No, but I found this," Laura said.

Mama glanced over her shoulder. She stood perfectly still, her eyes on the glove, her hand still holding the kettle. Then she turned back to the counter. "Please check his bicycle, Laura," she said in a level voice. "I must have those lids right now."

Laura put the glove on the table and went outside. Ryan's bike and jacket were lying on the grass under the maple tree. The jar lids were in the side pocket, along with some change. Without a word, Mama rinsed the lids and screwed them on tight. She wiped the jars with a damp cloth, then stood on a chair to set them on the top shelf of the cupboard.

The glove was still on the table when Ryan came in. He saw it right off.

"Why, Ryan?" Mama asked, and then her face crumpled. She covered it with her hands and sank into a chair. She didn't make a sound. She just sat there, while Ryan stood fingering his shredded glove and Laura stared at the floor, wanting all the bad stuff out and done with now.

After a while Laura drew a long, wavery breath and said, "He did the garden, too."

Mama finally straightened and ended the awful silence. "That's right, isn't it, Ryan? You did do the garden? And the buttons?"

Ryan hesitated, then nodded.

"Why?"

"Because . . ." Ryan cleared his throat. "Because I hate this place. I don't want to stay here."

"You thought a dead bird and some missing buttons would scare us away?"

"I . . ."

"Or was that just the beginning? Were you planning more?" Mama's careful voice carried no threat of tears or anger.

"I didn't know what else to do." Laura could barely hear Ryan, but Mama seemed to have no trouble.

"Other than ruin your glove," she reminded him. "Were you planning to leave that around as evidence of another vicious attack?"

Ryan shook his head. "I just don't need it anymore," he mumbled.

Mama sighed heavily and stood up. "We all have our disappointments, Ryan, but there are five people in this family and we have to act according to what's best for everybody." She laid her hand against his cheek for a moment, then went to the refrigerator and took out hot dogs and potato salad for supper. "You pick some lettuce to put this on, Laura," she said, "and you set the table, Ryan."

Laura went out into the warm evening as though she'd been let loose from a cage. She couldn't believe that was the end of it, and it wasn't. The next afternoon Ellen Davis drove up, and as she wasn't due to come again until September at the earliest, Laura knew Mama must have called her. Laura stayed up in the doorway of the hayloft until Ellen left and it was time to go down for chores.

"Ellen thinks Ryan needs help," Mama announced as soon as they all sat down for supper. "She's going to talk to some people and see what she can arrange. In the meantime, she's taking Ryan to meet the Redfield soccer coach, and she thinks he should try out for the drama club."

"I can't act," Ryan protested, but it didn't sound like an outright refusal to Laura.

"Yes, you can, Ryan, you're real good," she said, and surprised herself as well as her brother by giving him the extra ear of corn.

Daddy didn't say much until he'd finished

eating. "Miz Davis may have good ideas, I'm not saying she don't," he said as he pushed his plate back. "But we got troubles in our family, we don't wait on others to fix them. Ryan can play-act or kick a soccer ball here to kingdom come if that's what he wants, but he's not going to spend one more minute in front of that damn TV." He fixed his gaze squarely on Ryan. "Tomorrow morning I want you out there helping Luther with the raking, and when you're done with that you check in with me." Ryan, Laura was relieved to see, had the good sense to look agreeable.

"Now Dan," Mama said, but Daddy raised his hand and shook his head. "Don't you start, Franny," he said. "Keeping busy with what needs doing is the best medicine I know, and with Turner gone there sure is a hell of a lot to do around here."

"All right, Daniel, from now till school that's between you and Ryan and you don't need to speak rough about it." Mama pressed her lips primly together and said no more.

"I'll catch for you evenings," Luther spoke up for the first time. "You keep that pitching arm in shape, and I'll see you get to wherever there's a team playing next season."

Laura saw Ryan's head snap up. He knew as well as any of them, if you wanted to do something like sports you had to get yourself there and back. But Luther never made a promise he wouldn't keep, and Daddy didn't say a word as Luther pushed back from the table and went up to his room. This time he left his door open. When Laura went up later, she saw him sitting in the corner on his floor cushions. He was working on something in the bright circle of light from the lamp set on the floor next to him.

"Luther?" Laura said from the doorway. "What're you doing?"

Luther glanced up, startled, and straightened to look over the light into the gloom beyond. "Hi, Laurie-bell," he said, then went back to his work.

"Can I see what you're doing?" Laura asked again.

"Sure, I guess so." When she got close, Laura saw he had a small block of wood in his hand. He'd just started rounding and shaping it with the Swiss Army knife Uncle Ed had given him last Christmas.

"What's it going to be?" she asked.

"Oh, I don't know, it sort of comes along as I work." Luther moved over on the cushion so Laura could sit down. She watched the wood curl back from the knife and listened to her brother's breathing, like a tuneless whistle when he was concentrating on something he liked.

"Do you think Ryan will be okay?" she asked after a while.

"Yep, I do." Luther answered as if it were a sure thing. "Squeaky wheel gets the grease. Guess old Ryan dressed up that squeak some, and maybe we were a bit hard of hearing." Luther blew the shavings away and studied what he had done. With his eyes still on the wood, he said unexpectedly, "I want to thank you for that map, Laura. There's nothing wrong with *your* hearing."

So Luther *had* gone to Loria. "Didn't you love it, Luther? Isn't it beautiful? It's the most special thing I ever had. Did you see the tree? Did you see the throne where the roots separate off?" Laura rushed on in the excitement of sharing her secret treasure. "Sometimes I sit on the throne, sometimes I sit up in the branches.

It always feels good—like no matter how bad things seem, everything *really* is all right."

Laura hesitated. "I want Ryan to be happy, Luther, but I don't want to take him there. Do you think that's wrong?"

"No," Luther said gently. "No, Laura, not at all. It probably wouldn't mean the same thing to Ryan, just like playing baseball is no big deal to you or me."

Laura nodded with relief, and Luther concentrated again on his carving. She didn't mention the wooden deer she'd seen, lying on their sides on top of his crate. They were carved so carefully, she could tell they were fawns. She could even make out tiny hooves on the legs that lay severed from the little bodies. Luther must have known she'd see them. They were right out there on the crate, and he'd left his door open.

12

IT WAS AS THOUGH RYAN'S troubles had been a blister infecting the Cate family spirit, which, while shocking to discover, lost its venom when exposed and treated. Everyone was in a mood to enjoy the Addison County Fair.

Ralph Turner had hung rows of ribbons from past fairs along the wall above the bulk tank, and he didn't expect there to be any gaps now. Before leaving for Oregon, he'd taken care of all the entry details and left careful instructions for Daddy to follow. He even wrote down just what Luther, who would be staying with the cows and showing them, should wear.

Mama entered a jar of her zucchini relish and a maple walnut chiffon pie she'd been experimenting with. "Not one word, any of you," she warned when she decided on her final recipe, though none of them had the slightest idea of what was in it. Laura would never tell Mama she hadn't been able to taste the difference in the last few versions. All she knew was that maple walnut chiffon pie was no longer one of her favorites.

At the last minute, Laura entered a flower arrangement. She'd been sitting in the godmother tree, imagining, as she sometimes did, people who had come there in the past, all the way back to Indians pulling their canoes onto the little beach to rest in its shade. It didn't matter how long the tree had really been there; in Laura's mind it had existed forever, and without any planning at all she set about representing it at the fair. Wild asters, black-eyed Susans, and goldenrod; she picked some of every flower she could find, then laced and feathered the bouquet with field stalks and grasses and one sprig of leaves from the tree. She wrapped the stems in handfuls of wet vegetation she pulled from the swampy area beyond the beach, and hurried home to put the whole thing in the same jug she'd used for Luther's bouquet. She trailed vines around and around the jug, and finally wove a grass mat to set it on.

"What do you think, Mama?" Laura asked as she carefully put the arrangement on the kitchen table. "I'm going to enter it in the fair."

"Why, Laura." Mama walked slowly around the table, staring at the exuberant tangle of field and tree. "It's most . . . unusual" was all she could manage, but her voice made Laura smile with satisfaction.

"Yes." She nodded. "It worked out just right. Now I've got to write a label and figure how to keep it from tipping in the truck."

Rain in the night washed the dust from the grass and haze from the sky to leave the day of the fair clean and sparkling. The Cates—except for Luther, who had gone the night before—left right after the morning milking. Granger stayed behind in charge of the farm, coming to the edge of the road to wave after them as they drove away. Laura took some of the money she'd earned unloading and stacking hay bales; she'd already decided to buy licorice for Granger if she could find any. He liked the long chewy laces better than the candy sticks, but he thought licorice of any kind was a treat.

They brought Luther a thermos of coffee and some doughnuts. The cattle were already being judged: Sheba looked serenely confident of success, Hyacinth seemed more interested in Laura's opinion than the judge's, and the heifer Lulu flirted with everyone in sight. Laura thought if the handler's appearance counted for anything, Luther in his white pants and shirt was the clear winner.

The cows triumphed on their own merits, however. Sheba won an award for production, while Hyacinth took a ribbon for conformation, and the heifer for showing and fitting. Daddy and Luther were beaming, and Laura was free to go off on her own, with a reminder from Mama not to talk to strangers and not to take her eyes off her money for one split second.

Figuring the rides would get more crowded later in the day, Laura decided to start at the midway. For the first time in her life, she went on every single ride she wanted to, visiting the game booths in between. While Laura was willing to pay for the rides, she stayed at the edges of the games to watch other people play. One man, after just three questions, guessed people's occupations with such accuracy, Laura wondered why customers seemed so confident they could stump him. Other people threw pennies at squares or tossed rings at posts, which apparently wasn't as easy as it looked.

Laura's favorite game, though, was the tall pole with a bell at the top. People tried to ring the bell by hitting a pad at the bottom, which shot a little cylinder up a track. Every time the cylinder fell short of ringing the bell, onlookers would groan and the customer would examine the mallet for defects. One fat man took off his shirt, rolled his neck and shoulders to warm up, then with three mighty blows rang the bell each time. As he smiled to the applause and buttoned his shirt, a thin woman with silver-streaked hair stepped up and rang the bell with each of her three tries. The crowd cheered and laughed. The fat man looked for a second as if he'd been hit by the mallet, then grinned and joined the applause.

Laura saved the Ferris wheel until last. It was the one ride she didn't want to share with a stranger, and there were already enough people in line for everybody to have to double up. The only other time she'd been on a Ferris wheel, the girl who'd shared her seat had screamed and sobbed in such terror, Laura had been torn between feeling bad for the girl and embarrassed for herself. The ride attendant was the only one in the entire fairgrounds unaware of the problem. He had let the ride complete its course, as he lounged against the fence looking everywhere but at them.

Laura stepped out of line to take one last tour of the games. If she had to share a ride, she could certainly do better than the sticky boy ahead of her with the huge puff of cotton candy or the one behind in the spike necklace and the nose pin. She saw a familiar Red Sox T-shirt and headed for it. Ryan was with a boy he'd known when they'd lived at the Blairs'. A baseball pennant dangled from his hip pocket, and other prizes—a rolled poster, a rubber spider, and a green monster mask—lay in the dirt near his feet.

Laura stood back as he hurled three baseballs through a hole in a canvas backdrop. "Okay, kid, take your pick and get outta here," the hawker said with a lapse in his oily charm. The dart game Ryan wanted was for display only, the man told him.

"Liar," Laura muttered loudly enough for people to hear. "Dirty cheater." Ryan turned and saw her, then pointed to something up in the back corner. The man hesitated, then handed it over and launched into his come-on pitch. Laura was pleased to see that for the moment he had no takers. "You want this?" Ryan thrust into Laura's arms the huge white bear with an "I love you" heart he'd chosen.

"You mean it?" Laura stood looking from the the bear to Ryan and back again. She could hardly get her arms around the thing, it was so big. In spite of the size, it was cuddly soft and had a face that made her glad they'd rescued it from a man like that. "You mean it?" she said again. "I can keep it?"

"Sure. What would I want with it?" Ryan started to turn away with his friend.

"Ryan, wait a minute. Will you go on the Ferris wheel with me? I'll pay, I got enough. I just don't want to get stuck with some goober."

"Meet you by the videos," Ryan told his

friend. "Come on, Laura. There'd better not be a long line."

It was a tight squeeze getting the bear into the seat between them. After the ride, Laura lugged it back to the parking lot to leave with the rest of their stuff. She didn't take one of the sandwiches Mama had made; she figured she had just enough money left for Granger's licorice and a piece of chicken from the barbecue over by the auction tent.

The rest of the afternoon Laura wandered from the riding competition to the tractor pull to the fiddlers' show and clog dancing. In a field behind the fiddlers, a mob of kids scrambled to keep a great bubble of a ball in the air. Laura watched as it bobbled and bounced in slow motion, compared to the frantic efforts of its supporters. Suddenly the ball lolloped her way, and she dove to heave it up. "Good one," called a girl Laura had seen on the Redfield school bus, and Laura ran with the group, her head back and arms ready to give a boost, until it was time to make one last visit before they had to leave for home.

On her way past the craft and food exhibits, Laura noticed Mama's pie had been cut into and decorated with a red ribbon. The flower arrangements were the last aisle over. The entries looked as if they had come from florist shops. On one side, cut garden flowers posed in perfect designs, and on the other side dried flowers were arranged into baskets and wreaths and wall sprays.

Laura's bouquet stood by itself at the end of the cut flower table. A blue ribbon with SPECIAL CATEGORY stamped in gold at its center was stapled to a hand-written certificate that read:

Awarded for Beauty and Originality to
LAURA CATE
Lakeview Farm
Redfield, Vermont

CHAPTER

13

ROSE DIED NEAR THE END of August. What Daddy had thought was scours turned out to be a deformity of her digestive system. Daddy was sympathetic, but Laura knew he was also relieved they didn't have to worry about the other calves getting sick.

Even though Elsbeth took little notice of her baby's death, it comforted Laura to pour first her grief, then her good memories of the little calf, into the mother's ear as she brought the herd in for milking in the afternoons. It also helped that Granger, without saying a word, took over watering the other calves for a while.

Laura's eleventh birthday was two days before school started. Her usual excitement was dulled by Rose's death and by the thought of facing Miss Dunbar's class so soon, but after breakfast she packed a lunch, a book, her colored pens, and a roll of paper into her backpack and headed for Loria. Mama, who'd been bustling about with little private smiles, blew kisses after her. "Have a good day, dear," she called. "Don't be late for chores. We hope to finish early tonight."

Loria already reflected the ending summer. By late morning the sun was still trying to warm away the mists of the night. Some birch leaves had yellowed and dropped to float in patches at the mouth of the brook, and Laura found one scarlet leaf blazing in the grass under the godmother tree.

Laura settled into the warm hollow of the roots with her book, but her eyes drifted from its pages. In a way, she didn't even have Ryan to be new at school with. Ryan had taken to soccer with his usual passion for sports. He'd been riding his bike the five miles to and from practice for two weeks now, and though he'd never played soccer in his life, he already had a starting position on the team. The coach had even found a ride to the end of Valley Road for him after the regular season started. Being that good at sports was a free ticket to any school. There wasn't any such easy "in" for Laura. All sixth grade had was gym—not that she was a star at anything, except maybe running.

Luther wasn't going back, no matter how Mama pleaded and Ellen reasoned. Laura could understand why he was whistling over there in his room every night, carving away on something he wouldn't let her see.

Gradually the tightness in Laura's chest began to loosen, as it always did under the tree's spell. Like it or not, she was going to school the day after tomorrow. It might not be so bad. Loria would still be there, she could always talk to Riley, and that girl she'd seen at the fair looked nice.

After eating her lunch, Laura took her drawing stuff and went to sit up behind the wild rose thicket. The sun warmed her back as she bent over the paper, drawing the tangle with Elsbeth standing off to one side, and Rose peering out through the brambles the way she had the day Laura found her. In the background, she made the lake spread blue under the lower branches of the godmother tree.

Laura waited for the ink to dry before she carefully rolled the picture and started home. Her drawings, beginning with the one of the nightmare she'd had the first night in Redfield, now almost covered three walls in her room. In a while Mama wouldn't have to fret about wallpaper at all.

Ryan was missing chores and her birthday dinner for a scrimmage, but even so they finished in the barn in record time, as Uncle Ed showed up to lend a hand. Uncle Ed was as much a part of their birthday dinners as cake and candles, and his arrival sparked Laura's excitement. "Come on, princess," he said, propelling her across the road under his big arm. "Let's get this party going!"

"Here she comes!" Mama shouted, and Laura looked up to see Gramma Ryan standing next to her in the open door.

"Gramma!" she screamed, dashing up the steps to smother her with hugs and kisses. "I can't believe it. Are you going to stay? Do you like it here? Did you see my room? Don't you love the view? Wait till you see the sunset! I'll show you . . ."

"You won't show her anything if you don't stop squeezing the breath out of her," Mama said as she delivered a birthday kiss of her own. Gramma laughed and repinned her hair, and Uncle Ed beamed with the honor of having delivered the best present of all.

"Could hardly believe it myself," he said. "She called yesterday morning and said she'd like to come this way for a few days when it was convenient for me to fetch her. With Barbara away at her sister's, I was plumb relieved to have an escort for this event."

They ate barbecued chicken, corn on the cob, mashed potatoes, and salad, just as Laura had requested, with chocolate cake and peppermint ice cream for dessert. After supper they went in to the living room for Laura to open her presents: school clothes from Mama and Daddy, a lilac-colored clock radio from Uncle Ed and Aunt Barbara, and mittens and socks that Gramma had knit.

When the other things had been opened, Gramma took from her knitting bag a package wrapped in brown paper. "I wrote Alice after your visit, and she sent this for you. She doesn't have your Redfield address."

The paper felt strange, thicker and rougher than their brown wrapping paper. Inside was a sweater, soft and silky as Rose. It was knit in an Indian design of white, black, and brown.

"Dear Laura," read the attached note. "This sweater was knit by a woman in the knitting cooperative here. They use the alpaca wool from their own animals. I hope it brings you warmth. Love, Aunt Alice." Tucked into the fold of the sweater was a picture of Alice standing arm in arm with another woman. Both wore skirts and shawls decorated with designs like the one on the sweater. All Laura could see of their faces were wide smiles beneath the shadows cast by their wide-brimmed hats. In the background a road twisted steeply up in a barren-looking landscape.

"Well, my goodness, what got into Aunt Alice?" Mama said, but her eyes were gentle as she handed the sweater around. "I'm not partial to wool myself, but that's more like silk. Feel that, Daniel, you ever felt anything like that?"

Uncle Ed got the atlas from under the TV

and found the place in Peru that was printed on the sweater's label. "You'd need all the sweaters you could get when the sun goes down at that altitude," he said as he pointed out the spot on the map.

Laura studied the picture again. Where did that road go? It coiled like a snake rising to a charmer's whistle. She wished she could see more of Aunt Alice's face. The last time she'd visited, Laura had been sick with chicken pox. All she remembered of an earlier visit was feeling safe and happy sitting next to her on Gramma's sofa and admiring her bright red-and-purple skirt. She would write a thank-you letter, telling about the farm and about Loria, and maybe later she would write about school. It didn't look like Aunt Alice would get much mail in that place. Maybe she'd write back.

When Uncle Ed had gone and Laura was upstairs putting her gifts away, Luther came into her room. "I've got something for you, Laurie-bell," he said as he handed her a square box. "It's kind of between you and me." He leaned against the wall while she opened it, his dark eyes taking in the picture she'd made that afternoon and just finished tacking up.

Inside the box, packed in cotton from Mama's vitamin-pill bottle, Laura found two carved fawns. This pair had perfect legs prancing in play. "I've already started one of Rose," Luther said.

The next day was busy with Gramma and a last-minute trip into Redfield for notebooks and school sneakers. Laura had just enough time when they got back for one last trip to Loria before facing school. The afternoon was overcast, with a tang of fall in the air. Laura hoped the next day would be as cool, but even if it dawned ninety degrees hot, she was going to wear Aunt Alice's sweater.

She sat on her throne and let herself feel how keyed up she was. She was nervous about school, but it was an excited kind of nervous, not the dreading she had felt just yesterday. She had a lot more school to go if she was going to be a doctor like Aunt Alice . . . or maybe a vet . . . or one of those scientists who know about plants. She was going to travel, maybe even to some of the places Aunt Alice visited, helping cure sickness or figuring what would grow on rocky ground like she'd seen in the picture. She would have friends all over.

Laura sank back into the warm curve of the trunk. New places. New people. Like Redfield, like Tuttles' and Blairs' and all the other places they'd lived.

Laura watched the scudding clouds trail their skirts across the choppy water. The leaves above her whispered urgently. Laura listened intently for a moment, and then she smiled. If she remembered to look, she knew she could find her godmother tree anywhere.